Praise for

LAUNCH YOUR INNER ENTREPRENEUR

"Charlene Walters offers actionable advice to help female entrepreneurs build their confidence, manage their time, and find the resilience they need to make it through tough times. If you're serious about growing your business, *Launch Your Inner Entrepreneur* will help you get there!"

> **—Barbara Corcoran,** Shark & executive producer of
> ABC's *Shark Tank* and founder of The Corcoran Group

"Charlene Walters has created the perfect guidebook to help every aspiring female entrepreneur and business owner develop the entrepreneurial mindset necessary to launch and grow their startup and thrive in business."

> **—Jason Feifer,** editor-in-chief, *Entrepreneur* magazine

"When it comes to becoming a successful entrepreneur, so much of it has to do with developing the right attitude. Charlene Walters has put together an amazing book to help women on their journeys to becoming flourishing business owners by adopting the entrepreneurial mindset."

> **—Jon Steinberg,** founder of Cheddar News Channel and
> president of Altice News & Advertising

"Part entrepreneurship playbook, part women's empowerment guide, *Launch Your Inner Entrepreneur* is full of hacks to help female founders push boundaries in business and life. Intermingled with tips and motivation, Charlene Walters also serves up some laughs along the way. A must-read for fempreneurs."

> **—Christine Michel Carter,** senior contributor, ForbesWomen
> and the #1 global voice for working moms

"When it comes to entrepreneurship, mindset is a critical factor in success. Charlene Walters is the first to identify all of the common trouble spots for women entrepreneurs—and to offer actionable solutions that really work to overcome each problem area. This indispensable guidebook will equip and empower women in business with the mental strategies they need to beat the odds, creating a startup that grows and thrives. Highly recommended!"

> **—Robin Madell,** contributing writer, *Business Insider* and
> *U.S. News & World Report*

"Charlene Walters has delivered an essential tool for women everywhere who want to unleash their entrepreneurial spirit. Entrepreneurship is a mindset, and Charlene takes a practical, educational, and entertaining approach to helping women develop the mindset they need to succeed at the highest level."

> **—Jeff Hoffman,** serial entrepreneur from Priceline.com, Booking.com, and uBid.com; chairman of the Global Entrepreneurship Network

"Smart and timely, *Launch Your Inner Entrepreneur* helps women step up, take initiative, and grab their spot as savvy entrepreneurs! Kudos to Charlene Walters for compiling this engaging and enlightening book for women everywhere."

> **—Liz Montgomery,** author, *Oprah Magazine* insider and consultant

"In a positive and relatable way, Charlene Walters acts as a mentor and motivator, delivering just the push needed to help women kick ass along their entrepreneurial path! I highly recommend *Launch Your Inner Entrepreneur*!"

> **—Dawnmarie Deshaies,** CEO, author, and *New York Weekly* top 15 podcaster of 2020

"I want to give a copy of this book to every woman entrepreneur I have worked with. Charlene Walters doesn't just focus on what holds us back as women entrepreneurs; she shares with us real-life examples of how to overcome these hurdles. This book is inspiring!"

> **—Jennifer Murphy,** director, Connecticut Center for Entrepreneurship & Innovation

10 Mindset Shifts for Women to Take Action, Unleash Creativity, and Achieve Financial Success

LAUNCH

Your

Inner

ENTREPRENEUR

CHARLENE WALTERS, MBA, PHD

New York   Chicago   San Francisco   Athens   London   Madrid
Mexico City   Milan   New Delhi   Singapore   Sydney   Toronto

1 2 3 4 5 6 7 8 9   LCR   26 25 24 23 22 21

ISBN   978-1-264-25916-8
MHID   1-264-25916-6

e-ISBN   978-1-264-25917-5
e-MHID   1-264-25917-4

This publication is designed to provide accurate and authoritative information in regard to the subject matter covered. It is sold with the understanding that neither the author nor the publisher is engaged in rendering legal, accounting, securities trading, or other professional services. If legal advice or other expert assistance is required, the services of a competent professional person should be sought.
                    —*From a Declaration of Principles Jointly Adopted by a Committee of the*
                    American Bar Association and a Committee of Publishers and Associations

Library of Congress Cataloging-in-Publication Data

Names: Walters, Charlene, author.
Title: Launch your inner entrepreneur : 10 mindset shifts for women to take action, unleash creativity, and achieve financial success / Charlene Walters, MBA, PhD.
Description: New York : McGraw Hill Education [2021] | Includes bibliographical references and index.
Identifiers: LCCN 2020047145 (print) | LCCN 2020047146 (ebook) | ISBN 9781264259168 (hardback) | ISBN 9781264259175 (ebook)
Subjects: LCSH: Businesswomen. | New business enterprises. | Women-owned business enterprises. | Entrepreneurship. | Success in business.
Classification: LCC HD62.5 .W354 2021 (print) | LCC HD62.5 (ebook) | DDC 658.1/1082—dc23
LC record available at https://lccn.loc.gov/2020047145
LC ebook record available at https://lccn.loc.gov/2020047146

McGraw Hill books are available at special quantity discounts to use as premiums and sales promotions or for use in corporate training programs. To contact a representative, please visit the Contact Us pages at www.mhprofessional.com.

For my two beautiful daughters (and future entrepreneurs), Avery and Tegan. May you always fill your lives with happiness, success, and love.

CONTENTS

TAKE ACTION

One day, you will be happily working for someone else: exceeding monthly goals and growing their profits. And then, another day, you'll realize that you're not getting the recognition or opportunities that you deserve. It's at *that* moment that you'll wonder why the heck you're doing this to yourself and—*bam!*—your entrepreneurial lightbulb will begin to glow.

Are you a woman who wants to take control of your earnings and your life? Are you dissatisfied with the corporate grind and want to follow your passions professionally? Are you tired of getting paid less than your peers for doing the same work? I've been there before, and I know what you're experiencing.

Perhaps you've already struck out on your own as an entrepreneur, or maybe you hope to do so in the near future. It's a big jump either way, and you'll need extra support to give it your best shot. If you're like many women (myself included), you are also the primary breadwinner in your household and have a burning desire to bring in additional income for your family. I don't blame you: you want to take care of them and give them the best.

If any of these statements ring true, then this is the book for you and *now* is the time to take action, as there will be many new business opportunities for female entrepreneurs resulting from morphing industries in the aftermath of COVID-19. You deserve this chance!

You won't be alone, either—more women are starting businesses than ever before. In fact, 42 percent of all small business or franchise owners are women, and there are *13 million female-owned businesses contributing to $1.9 trillion in revenue.*[1] Current trends suggest it's likely these numbers will keep rising—so it's time for you to grab your share of the revenue, and today is the day to get started.

Your transformation will begin in the mind. After all, entrepreneurship is an inside job. If you're a woman who is ready to take the plunge into becoming a company founder, then there are important mental shifts that you must make before you kick off your journey. You must put aside your insecurities and doubts about the success or failure of your venture, as well as the fears associated with no longer receiving a steady paycheck, so that you can move forward to become an effective business owner.

This is a tall order, but taking action is the first of 10 Mindset Shifts you'll read about in this book that you must embrace as a "fempreneur" (a female entrepreneur) if you not only want to make that initial entrepreneurial leap, but also hope to continue to grow and expand your business over time—launching your inner entrepreneur and unleashing the startup within.

Why Now?

Of the many reasons that women decide to pursue entrepreneurship, a key one is dissatisfaction with corporate life. According to a recent study, "over the past five years, the number of women in senior leadership has grown. Still, women continue to be underrepresented at every level."[2] Consequently, many women have opted out of corporate jobs to become their own bosses, accounting for the growing rate at which women are launching businesses over the past 25 years. As more women become company founders, though, they face common challenges along the path as new business owners—challenges that they can mitigate by understanding how to shift from a corporate mindset, where much of the necessary action is laid out for you behind the scenes, to an entrepreneurial mindset in which you are the main driver of the action and must chart your own course.

It's really about figuring out what it means to *actually become* an entrepreneur and then executing on that—and today, this begins with understanding the shifting business models that companies are now trying to make sense of. The number of entrepreneurial women will undoubtedly keep rising as a result of lost jobs through conventional employment, furloughs, and other transitions that may affect employment status. In fact, a disproportionate percentage of women (80 percent vs. 20 percent men) left the workforce due to being impacted by COVID-19.[3] In tandem, as automation and artificial intelligence become more of the corporate norm, women's professional journeys will begin to morph as well. The convergence of these trends, along with the continued underrepresentation of women in corporate leadership roles, creates a perfect storm for traditional employment to decrease for women and entrepreneurial opportunities to correspondingly rise.

These changes in the world of work bring us to you, in this moment, and what you can do to take the initiative rather than be a victim of what's happening in companies globally—how you can take charge of your destiny rather than becoming a statistic of the latest round of corporate cuts. The current massive shifts in the labor landscape suggest that *today is the day to make a move on your entrepreneurial inklings*.

It Starts in Your Mind

As an entrepreneurship mentor who has worked closely with countless female entrepreneurs, I can testify from firsthand experience that for women, there is so much about becoming an entrepreneur that begins with transforming the way you think. Research shows that many women suffer from deficits in confidence and feel more doubt and insecurity about their abilities and talents than men do—insecurities that can hold them back from ever starting down the entrepreneurial path.[4] So let's begin by talking about the mindset adjustment required for a woman to become a true entrepreneur. Are you ready? I hope so.

Desire is half the battle. To remain successful in a world where traditional employment will become less frequent, you'll do well to focus on those areas where you excel and tasks you love to do. You'll also need to keep learning and growing throughout your journey, because technological and industry advances will only escalate in frequency and speed. That means your learning and skill attainment must become more rapid and consistent as well.

All of this momentum pushing women toward an entrepreneurial life is a great thing. You'll be doing more of what you really enjoy and less of what you don't, which is in line with the fact that the pursuit of passion is one of the main reasons that women dive into entrepreneurship in the first place.[5] The increased focus on learning and mindset adjustment associated with starting your own business will keep you fresh and challenged, too. So, it's time to start thinking about what skills you'll need to gain, and how you can shift your mindset to facilitate the life of a successful fempreneur.

Taking Action

A Mindset Shift related to taking action will be central to your success in terms of not only having the confidence to get your business off the ground, but also in regard to what you'll need to do every single day to keep moving your business forward. Taking action is a key component of an entrepreneurial mindset. Thriving female business owners are doers, not merely dreamers (although I do encourage you to aim high). This Mindset Shift will show you a few of the ways you can take action and get started.

Getting Ready to Flip the Switch

Motivation to become an entrepreneur is one piece of the puzzle for women who aspire to be company founders. But a mental switch must flip in your brain when it comes to *actually becoming* an entrepreneur—a switch that, once activated, will trigger changes in your thinking and behavior, helping to create an entrepreneurial mindset that propels you to action. You must be ready to embrace the power of this new way of thinking to catapult your career in a more independent direction.

With your decision to launch a company, you jump-start your life, your earnings, and your potential. Founding a startup also gives you a chance to create a business that exactly matches your values, vision, passion, and expertise.

Rather than taking this ability for granted, consider whether it makes sense in your career and your life to seek a more innovative path. Do you want to embrace this power to make a move and seize control of your own destiny? If you heard your mind screaming "Yes!" as you read that question, then your independence may be just around the corner. It all starts with a desire and a plan—the pace and practice of the Mindset Shift is up to you. *You've got this, girl.*

Starting as a Side Hustle

While taking action is your ultimate goal, you don't have to jump headfirst into it without a trial run. The path of a fempreneur requires a huge career commitment, which is why beginning with a gig or "side hustle" while you're still traditionally employed is a smart way to test the waters. A recent study found that more than 44 million Americans have some sort of side gig.[6] Further, 51 percent of the women surveyed had side hustles compared to only 35 percent of the men surveyed.[7]

What are the benefits of this more measured approach? Establishing a side hustle provides aspiring fempreneurs with both the security of a stable income and the freedom to experiment with growing a company separate from their day job. Building your business more slowly after hours while still working full-time can take the financial pressure off, allowing you to continue to bring in pay while potentially growing your venture's revenue at the same time. If and when you're financially and emotionally ready to turn your side gig into full-time entrepreneurship, *then* you can quit your day job. A side hustle is how I got started, a little at a time.

There are countless possible launching pads for a side hustle that you can grow into a full-time business, such as teaching, writing, digital marketing, tutoring, coaching, child care, pet care, AI, IT, training, product development, photography, real estate, and graphic design. You might also consider food preparation, catering, cleaning, repair services, landscaping, market research, event planning, house-sitting, beautician/stylist services—the list goes on depending on your own skills, interests, and expertise, and is limited only by your imagination. Do you like to work with people, throw virtual parties, or create things? Are you eager to showcase your writing talent? Consider where you can provide the most value while reaping the highest reward. What better way to develop yourself than to start a company? And I would add that there is no smarter way to reach that goal than greasing the wheels for it with a well-planned side hustle.

Finding Your Niche

Part of flipping the switch to an entrepreneurial mindset involves finding an appropriate focus for your business. Research has found that one of the main reasons small businesses fail is a lack of understanding of their target audience.[8] Aspiring fempreneurs must recognize the essential nature of investigating the market that they are considering by examining the competition, complementary products or services, and unmet needs. This type of specialization involves identifying a gap or doing something better than other companies serving the same business sector, which requires uncovering and eliminating customer pain points to create a more seamless experience for your target market.

Don't rely only on your online research. Talk to other market insiders for ideas, and remember that the goal is to serve your niche better than anyone else. A once-little startup disrupted the taxi and limousine industry by developing a deep understanding of an existing space and solving customer problems. Perhaps you've heard of it. Uber. By simplifying transportation for riders, Uber changed the way people get around and decimated the competition. If your car breaks down or you want a designated driver after a girls' night out, you can easily get to where you want to go or hit the town without having to deal with a rental car or taxi. Thanks to Uber, Lyft, Car2Go, Zimride, and the other disruptors that followed! It will be interesting to see what happens next in this morphing industry.

Once you've homed in on a potential niche, be sure to do even more fact-finding to ensure that there is a worthwhile market potential for your startup. Is there really a demand and desire for your product or service? Does anyone really *want* jalapeño-flavored chocolate chip cookies? You'll never know until you investigate.

As you consider possible areas of focus, you should also reflect on the amount of time you can commit to your startup and the competition you'll face. Look to other entrepreneurs who have similar businesses to assess if a particular angle is worth your while, and do some major digging. Let's face it, when women want to get to the bottom of something, we know how to investigate—Facebook, Instagram, Twitter, Google. I'm sure you know all about what your ex-boyfriend or girlfriend is up to now, just saying. (No judgment here.)

Learning About Your Target Market

Becoming more inquisitive so that you can get your target audience and product just right is a major part of the Mindset Shift we've been talking about—as well as your forward momentum as a fempreneur—so prepare to invest your energy heavily in this direction. It involves researching the big picture about who you hope to sell your products or services to. After identifying a niche for your startup, you must leverage an entrepreneurial mindset to continue doing your homework via market research, as the first few months after launch are vital. You'll need sales and customers as soon as possible, and doing the proper probing will ensure a steady stream.

As the key to laying a solid foundation for your new company, your goal should be to accurately identify target customers—in other words, your ideal audience—and where they congregate. As a fempreneur, you also need to understand your target customers' demographics, learn how much they are willing to pay for your product or service, figure out why they would buy from you, determine what type of messaging you should use to reach them, drill down into where they do business, and uncover what speaks to them. You'd be shocked at how many entrepreneurs neglect these basics!

Depending on your business, you might also want your market research to unearth answers such as what they had for lunch, what their favorite movie is, who they most admire, and what color socks they are wearing today—you can never know too much about your target customers. All right, maybe you don't really need to know that they were running late this morning and now have on one pink and one purple sock (unless you're planning to sell footwear), but it could be an interesting detail for you anyway.

The bottom line is that you must zero in on identifying opportunities or voids in the market. Think of big entrepreneurial success stories you've heard about, such as Spanx, Stitch Fix, Airbnb, and Amazon. They all began simply by doing something better than all of the other companies currently servicing an industry. Those then-startups—which are now behemoths in their industries—uncovered a pain point and eliminated it, making a more seamless experience for customers. Now we can flatten our stomachs without doing crunches, look fabulous in the clothes we had picked for us by our online stylist, as we rent out our houses and have anything we want delivered within a day—possibly by drone or robot—to our doorstep. What lucky women we are, thanks to the visionary entrepreneurs behind these companies.

What will *you* do to further simplify people's lives? That's a bottom-line question that should drive your market research and your entrepreneurial mindset in general. Train your mind to focus on figuring out what's required for your customers' ease. If you can make doing business with you painless by locating a source of friction or underserved desire—ideally one that aligns with your knowledge and pursuits—then you've got your business concept. Once you get into the process of revealing answers about your target market through research, you may find that more and more ideas start coming to you. You're flipping the switch as you develop the mindset of a startup founder.

When considering a market, you should also ask yourself if it is large enough to allow for significant growth in the future. Find out what other products or services are similar in the space. What percentage of the market share do competitors have? What portion can you realistically grab? Monique Lhuillier, fashion designer and entrepreneur, had the right mindset to achieve business success. She said, "I went looking for dresses and realized there was a niche I could fill in the wedding dress market."[9] This entrepreneurial mindset is also exhibited by Spanx founder Sara Blakely, who said, "Don't be intimidated by what you don't know. That can be your greatest strength and ensure that you do things differently from everyone else."[10]

But getting down to brass tacks, how do you actually get the information you need about your ideal audience so that you can learn what you need to know to best serve it? When looking for potential customers to survey, you can start by tapping existing connections, contacts, and friends from your email list or social media platform (Facebook, Twitter, and LinkedIn work well here). You can also explore the possibility of partnering with a company for survey distribution, going places where you might find your target audience, publishing an article or ad about your survey, or leveraging the services of a market research firm that will collect participants for you. I've successfully used all of these methods before and each have their merit. Explore all potential resources available to you to collect this valuable intel. Offer perks to incentivize people to take your survey too: gift certificates, SWAG giveaways, and more. I'm telling you, people will do just about anything for a free T-shirt! I'm sure you have a few of them in your closet . . . as do I.

When it comes to actually conducting your market research, there are a number of methods that you can utilize, including using surveys (in person, online, and via email) as mentioned; focus groups where a moderator conducts interviews with a group of five people or more; personal interviews during which the interviewer asks open-ended questions in a nonstructured way; observations, where consumers are observed interacting with products or services; and trials, where consumers test and provide feedback on an actual product. Surveys are often the easiest method to start with, and they can be a lot of fun for a new entrepreneur, too. It's exciting to be out there interacting with your potential customers, and if they express energy and enthusiasm about your offering, it can help give you an extra boost of motivation. It's also encouraging to watch your idea gain traction. I love it!

When using surveys for market research, ask customers and potential customers their age, gender, level of education, geographic location, job title, and income. You should also find out what competitive products or services they are currently purchasing (including the brand name), their level of satisfaction with their current product/service, and if they would purchase your product if it becomes available (be sure to ask why or why not). Also, try to uncover the price that they are willing to pay, what their hobbies and interests are, and where they currently look for information and hang out. You are going to want to hang out there too (unless they're at the dentist having their teeth cleaned—but even then, they are a captive audience). Pull it in and watch the excitement build—you're a fact-finding fempreneur now!

There are other steps involved too, which include developing a customer persona (we'll talk more about this later), scrutinizing your competitors, conducting a SWOT analysis, and undergoing proper product development and testing. You can identify and assess your competitors by looking at their websites, going to their stores or physical locations, ordering their products, and then comparing all of these factors in terms of strengths and weaknesses.

A SWOT analysis, an exercise where you outline the strengths, weaknesses, opportunities, and threats associated with your business relative to your three main competitors, will help with this sort of comparison. Product development and testing will be performed later, after you've gathered input from potential customers, developed your prototype, and then tested it. You can't adequately move into the planning stage that comes after market research until you've done these types of analyses. So do your homework, girl!

Prepping for Product Development

As entrepreneurs, we've got to uncover what consumers really want, not what they are telling us they want. With this mindset of discovery, and once you've completed your basic market research, you'll be able to move forward with your product development by creating an MVP, or minimum viable product. An MVP is the least complicated version of your product that you can build in order to attract and ascertain interest in it, and get feedback from potential customers so that you can perfect and improve the product before a full launch. When developing your MVP, think in terms of must-have features, functionality, and extra attributes that could delight your customers. Your product prototype should be refined enough so that consumers would be willing to buy or try it, and it should have enough bells and whistles to keep potential buyers interested.

An MVP provides a feedback circle to guide your product's future development, so that you're really providing exactly what customers want and value. Your MVP can be as simple as a website teaser page—which is an online page that describes and sells your product or service before it is available on the market—or it might be a demo of the product in person or via video. Test your MVP with hypothetical customers and adjust as necessary. The value of this step is emphasized by the words of Emily Weiss, founder and CEO of the billion-dollar beauty brand Glossier, who said, "I read every single comment that comes in."[11] You should too.

Use the MVP step as the final stage of your market research to gather as much information as you can in order to ensure that your product or service will be well received by your target audience. You want customers to be lined up at your front door waiting for it to launch! Can you picture them? I can.

Creating Your Business Plan

With the results of your market research in hand, it's now time to adopt a forward-thinking, proactive planning mindset. In the words of Eleanor Roosevelt, "It takes as much energy to wish as it does to plan."[12] She was a wise woman! If you began last year, your startup would already be up and running. Maybe you've already launched your business and it's time to move on to your next phase. Either way, start where you stand and build on it one small step at a time.

As you think about the big picture of your business, you'll want to figure out the answers to some key questions related to planning for your entrepreneurial future:

- How much do you want to make?
- Who can potentially help you—friends, relatives, a spouse/significant other?

- How quickly do you want to grow?
- What will your business ideally look like after six months or a year?
- What resources do you already have, and which must you acquire?

A formal business plan is a great place to start figuring out answers like these and mapping out the vision for your business. In it, you'll include a business summary, company synopsis, history, mission statement, revenue model, and an overview of the product or service. You'll also use your business plan to identify key features of the market, your company's management structure, industry trends, a competitive analysis, and financial projections, as well as your strategies for marketing, customer acquisition, social media, and public relations. If asking outside investors for money, you'll additionally include how much capital you require for starting up and how it will be allocated. When it comes to compiling all of this information, there's no need to reinvent the wheel—you can pull a free business plan template from online and use it to guide the process. This is where your friend Google can assist you. (Also see the Fempreneur Action Plan at the end of this book. It will help you outline some of the information needed for your business plan.)

While it may seem like a lot of effort to put in on the front end, a business plan is important for so many reasons. It can help identify potential pitfalls or holes in your strategy, aid in decision making, show how viable your business concept is, enable you to set more accurate goals and progress checks, reduce risks, help you obtain funding, and facilitate planning—all of which can give your entrepreneurial endeavor the best chance of success. Although you might feel like taking the time to write a business plan will slow you down from starting your company, this initial preparation is actually critical to your longevity and ultimate success as a fempreneur. Just because your grandma thinks you can do it, doesn't make it so (although we love her support). Planning will be essential. In the words of soccer sensation Mia Hamm, "The backbone of success is hard work, determination, good planning, and perseverance."[13]

Finding a Mentor

If you are struggling with any of the initial groundwork related to launching your business, it can help to seek a mentor. A recent study found that one of the biggest challenges female entrepreneurs must overcome is a lack of strong role models and mentors—so no matter how much of a go-getter you are, part of your entrepreneurial Mindset Shift needs to involve seeking help when you need it.[14] There are mentors available through the Small Business Administration (SBA), and you can even hire a consultant with expertise in business strategy and planning to mentor you. Look to people you admire in your network, too.

Keep in mind that selecting and asking someone to "be your mentor" can feel overwhelming in itself. It's sort of like asking someone to marry you after you've only just met. To be sure that a mentor is the right fit for you, request an hour of her time instead (paid or not). Come to the meeting prepared with specific questions, and get as much out of it as you can by proactively providing information about you and your company prior to the meeting.

Then circle back in a few months or so—after you've had a chance to see some preliminary results (sooner if needed)—and set up another appointment with your mentor. I'm a mentor through my own consulting company (http://www.charlenewalters.com) and on Entrepreneur's Ask An Expert platform (https://www.entrepreneur.com/ask-an-expert/), and I can tell you that entrepreneurship mentors really enjoy working with other entrepreneurs. Sometimes it just takes someone to bounce your ideas off of, and this can certainly be invaluable when it comes to your business planning and forward momentum. Look for a mentor whose personality, business, or goals align with your own. You can also gather additional information related to business planning from the National Association of Women Business Owners (NAWBO, https://www.nawbo.org/) and from the Office of Women's Business Ownership, which is part of the SBA (https://www.sba.gov/offices/headquarters/wbo).

Once you've finalized your business plan, you'll need to file the necessary registration and legal paperwork related to your company. You can find this type of information on the Staying Legally Compliant section of the SBA website (https://www.sba.gov/business-guide/manage-your-business/stay-legally-compliant). This practice ensures that you've done all of the homework critical to meeting your strategic goals and objectives. Your business plan lays the foundation for your startup, and all of the corresponding paperwork ensures that your company is legitimate and that you are following the laws and regulations connected with your industry and geographical location. It is always a smart practice to have an attorney help you with these tasks—and don't wait too long on this step; you'll want to do this in the beginning to avoid any potential legal or regulatory pitfalls down the road.

Funding Your Venture

Your niche is identified, market research conducted, MVP test-driven, and business plan finalized—now it's time to get into a money mindset! Your venture won't get far without a realistic budget and/or funding sources. Research has shown that many women struggle with money management: in one survey of 1,048 U.S. adults, "almost 40% of women said they feel 'overwhelmed' when thinking about their finances and 31% feel 'discouraged.' Meanwhile, only 9% of women reported feeling 'empowered' and only 8% said they felt 'excited.' In contrast, men were more likely than women to associate positive feelings with finances across the board. For example, men most frequently reported feeling 'in control' of their finances (42%) or 'hopeful' (33%)."[15] So, if you're among the women who are feeling overwhelmed or discouraged when it comes to the financial side of your business, then you'll need to work extra hard on this particular Mindset Shift.

Another study found that "female-owned businesses generally underperform male-owned businesses on a variety of measures such as revenue, profit, growth, and discontinuance [i.e., failure] rates."[16] This is another reason fempreneurs have to take steps to boost their financial confidence and savvy, and buck this disappointing trend.

Let's start with some basics. You must be able to financially back your venture or invest in certain activities to get it off the ground—and you will have to continually focus on this as a business owner. If seeking investors right off the bat feels intimidating, don't be too quick to disregard the option of self-funding or bootstrapping until you gain traction. Do as much as you can by yourself when you're first starting out to cut costs. Think about it like your thrifty college days when you ate ramen every day for a year to save your limited cash, or hunted for loose change under the couch cushions. (I bet you were thrilled when you found a five-dollar bill and a lost earring; we won't talk about the rest!)

You can also secure needed funds for your startup through a partnership, by taking on additional investors, or applying for a business loan or grant. (Check out the SBA's loans and grants for female business owners.) If you're going the investor route, keep in mind that any potential investors will want to see a detailed business plan and pitch before backing you, so make sure that you follow the steps presented here to get it ready before approaching prospective outside funders.

Some women get funding from friends or relatives, which can be a helpful way to obtain early assets—with one important caveat. Make sure that you take the proper precautions and put an agreement in place that spells out your plan for repayment and/or what each individual's stake is in the company as a result of their investment. I know that we want to trust our friends and family (and in general, we should), but omitting this legality by putting the details in writing up front can lead to strained relationships and misunderstandings down the line. Protect yourself and those you care about by requiring a signed agreement. You don't want Aunt Bessie demanding 50 percent of your first million after investing only $100 in your business!

Many women are even launching their companies through crowd-funding—and with impressive results. As Jen Earle, CEO of the NAWBO, notes,"Women have become very active in crowdfunding platforms. In fact, recent data on Kickstarter shows that on average, they are 9% more successful than men."[17] Kickstarter is leading the way as one of the most popular sites for this type of investment. As explained on their web-site, "Kickstarter campaigns make ideas into reality. It's where creators share new visions for creative work with the communities that will come together to fund them."[18] There are other popular crowdfunding sites too, like Indiegogo, Pozible, Fundly, and Fundable. Crowdfunding works bet-ter for some types of businesses (like tech gadgets, local business services, clever inventions, video games, and books) than others, so do your research and consider it if you think it might be a good fit.

Trying a Pitch Competition

You can get fun and creative about how you seek funding opportunities. For example, some women hock their ideas for brands in pitch competi-tions and on TV shows like "Entrepreneur Elevator Pitch" and "Shark Tank," where multiple participants vie for investor backing. In pitch wars like these, entrepreneurs come to the table armed with information related to their business concept, including their unique selling proposition (USP), target market, and overall marketing message and position. They also provide details related to their projected startup and funding costs, product development strategy, and other data derived from prior market research and early traction/interest.

Investors (or judges) in these competitions are usually looking for a solid product concept that is different from other currently existing products. As the "pitcher," you need to be able to explain your concept succinctly and clearly. Judges want to invest in a business that taps an unmet need in the market. Additionally, they look for early traction and a niche that is scalable and will grow over time. Finally, they want to see an entrepreneur who is knowledgeable, energetic, committed, and passionate about her product or service. These investors are investing in you as a person as much as your product or startup, so make sure you are someone whom they can see themselves partnering with. In the words of Body Shop founder Anita Roddick, "Whatever you do, be different. That was the advice my mother gave me, and I can't think of better advice for an entrepreneur. If you are different, you will stand out."[19] So, figure out an angle that makes you stand out from the crowd (in a good way) and work that into your pitch!

As you do so, remember to keep your pitch simple and straightforward, focusing only on the most relevant information and details. Don't underestimate the power of research here, too. Watch back episodes of pitch competitions to see which pitches worked, which didn't, and why. Find some good pitch templates of the many available online. Remember what you learned in preparing your business plan about focusing on holes in existing markets and using survey research to demonstrate how you might provide value and alleviate current pain points. Prepare, practice, and be willing to do the work.

Participating in business competitions can help women startup leaders boost their confidence, because the process of doing so not only helps them get their business plan in order, but also gives them practice selling their concept to others. A fempreneur must nail her elevator pitch and be comfortable explaining and talking about her company every day, and a pitch competition can kick-start that process. I was fortunate enough to accompany three female entrepreneurs whom I mentored when they presented their ideas on "Entrepreneur Elevator Pitch." I can say with all certainty that it was an extremely valuable learning experience for them (and for me too)!

There is no "right" approach for nailing a pitch competition. Preparation, a lot of which just comes down to common sense, is key for doing well, though. Have your facts together. Brainstorm and anticipate questions. Do your homework and practice, practice, practice. If you do everything as well as possible and still don't win, don't despair. Simply investing your time and energy into being a part of the competition helps to embed your entrepreneurial mindset. The feedback you receive, both positive and negative, can also help take your startup to the next level. So hold your head up high, no matter the outcome, because you come out ahead either way. Take it from Barbara Corcoran, a "Shark Tank" judge and investor who founded the real estate brokerage firm The Corcoran Group, which she sold to NRT for $66 million: "All the best things that happened to me happened after I was rejected. I knew the power of getting past no."[20]

Developing Your Skills

A learning mindset is essential in order to blossom as a female founder. As part of that mindset, you must teach yourself new skills or seek out those who can teach them to you. This will expand your knowledge and confidence. While you move forward on the journey to becoming an entrepreneurial thinker, it's important to focus on skill development to leverage everything that you bring to the table as a business trailblazer (yes, you!). Are you ready to harness the culmination of your charisma, abilities, knowledge, and talents to sell yourself, your brand, and your products to clients and potential investors?

This skill development is unique for each of us but so vital as a fempreneur. The fact is that people have a choice whether to do business with you over someone else. The best investment a woman can make is always in herself and growing her knowledge base, particularly as a startup owner. Your skill development is part of your own USP. It's what you'll use to sell yourself, your brand, and your products to clients and potential investors, and it encompasses all those things you know and can share with valuable stakeholders—like industry trends, market research, product and market knowledge, technical skills, your business acumen, and more. Your USP and continual growth should be at the forefront of your mind from the moment you become an entrepreneur and throughout your entire entrepreneurial career, as its development will add value to all of your interactions with customers. You can continue to grow your USP by reading books, industry articles, and journals; attending conferences, workshops, and webinars; and taking classes and networking to gather additional information and stay current.

Getting the Word Out

After working through the previous steps, I bet you're starting to feel the positive effects of the shift to a full-on fempreneur mindset mode. What's left is to start hustling and getting the word out about your business in a big way! It's time to set up your website and social media accounts and begin growing your brand presence. When you're just starting out, it's often simplest (and least expensive) to build your website using a ready-made template from a web-hosting company like GoDaddy or Wix. I built my website on GoDaddy and was very satisfied with the experience. It was simple to create, and I'm proud of it!

Ready-made templates keep your site looking professional, and there are plenty of options to choose from. To understand why setting up a company website is so critical, consider that it's like a virtual brochure for your product or service. It certainly makes you look more credible and legitimate if people can easily find you online. Further, a website is up and running 365 days a year, 24 hours a day, so potential customers can access it anytime—even while you're busy getting your beauty sleep. Having a website saves you time and helps you reach a broader audience. It allows you to present your product or service more quickly and efficiently, converting visitors into raving fans of your brand.

Some tips of the trade: Pay attention to the content that you put on your website and ensure that it's easy to find. You'll need to put some thought into navigation to ensure your site is intuitive and easy for visitors to interact with. Leverage customer ratings and testimonials when possible, as consumers rely heavily on these when making purchasing decisions—more so than any other factor, which I found out firsthand when I conducted a study on why people choose to purchase from one website versus another. Potential customers really do want to know what Helen from Montana thinks about your skin-care line. Did she give it four stars or five, and why? What did her skin look like after she used it? Did her husband notice (does he ever)?

Make sure that potential customers are also able to contact you easily after visiting your website by including several different methods to reach you: phone, email, postal owl (just kidding, this isn't Hogwarts!). Add videos and other multimedia content to help bring your site to life. Put yourself front and center in them, as you are a proud female business owner, and show people what you know and what you can do for them. Ensure that your site is mobile-friendly, and test it on multiple browsers and devices. This is where having a ready-made template will really come in handy, as that work has already been done on the back end.

Cultivating a Selling Mindset

Driving sales is of course one of the top goals of any entrepreneur, yet there's a specific Mindset Shift that must accompany this. As American business mogul Estée Lauder said, "I have never worked a day in my life without selling. If I believe in something, I sell it and I sell it hard."[21] To succeed in it, women must overcome the negative connotation that's often associated with sales. Once that happens, they can leverage the power of selling to provide value to consumers. Selling commonly ignites fear in women, but it is exactly what is needed to launch a business and grow it successfully. So, fempreneur, you must learn to overcome that fright and master your inner sales guru.

Some experts feel that women have a natural advantage in this arena. Women have many attributes that can often make them the top sales associates in organizations, which is great news for you.[22] I was a top sales associate at an import company early on in my career (and have the cheesy placards to prove it). It was such a valuable experience for me because selling is a skill that all entrepreneurs need to master, and that position enabled me to gain that particular talent.

There is no magic recipe for becoming a top sales performer, I promise. But you can't go wrong with being consistent, persistent, and personable. Make cold calls, prospect, and do whatever it takes to get your brand in front of potential clients. Even if they decline at first, many will eventually listen to you, if only to find out who has been contacting them so much.

How can you overcome the negative perception associated with sales? It all boils down to the mindset you adopt. Remind yourself that when it comes to the growth of your startup, selling is not bad; in fact, your business needs it to flourish. And, as a fempreneur, you are the main saleswoman for your company and have to create that sense of urgency or demand for your product. In the words of Marissa Mayer, CEO of Yahoo! Inc., "If you push through that feeling of being scared, that feeling of taking risk(s), really amazing things can happen."[23] If you're still not convinced, then don't think of yourself as a salesperson; think of yourself as *providing value to others*. You have an amazing product or service, and they need it to improve their lives. You're actually helping them. And you love to help other people, don't you? Why, I bet today you've already helped your child, a couple of coworkers, several clients, and maybe someone you don't even know. Research shows that helping and other prosocial behavior comes more naturally for many women.[24] So, if you love helping people, then channel that helping spirit into selling your business!

Preparation can ease your apprehension about sales (as well as reminding yourself that you're a trailblazing female leader now). To take the guesswork out of your sales calls, develop a brief sales script that you can use for contacting and interacting with potential customers. This will help you identify what you want to say and how. Practice your script over and over until it comes out naturally. Next, create a projected sales forecast and ascertain what it will take to reach your goals. As part of that process, formulate your plan for contacting customers. How will you identify prospects? How many calls or contacts will you make a day to achieve your benchmarks? What days and times will you devote to making these contacts?

Don't be all about closing the deal either. A big part of selling has to do with getting to know people, showing an interest in them, and being personable. It takes time to develop real relationships and trust with your customers. That's your advantage when you are starting out as a small fish in your industry—you can develop stronger connections and be much more responsive than larger competitors, and frankly, women are often better at it. Don't take rejection of your sales pitches personally; it's all part of the game. Remember that crush who broke your heart and how you were able to get over it and move on to your next crush (who was even better)? Same concept here.

When I sell, I pull out all of the stops. Once I even invented a goodie basket that was filled with all kinds of treats (branded swag, cookies, stuffed animals, and other indulgences)—alongside a sneaker with a stuffed sock in it. Sounds strange I know, but I would enclose a brochure and a note that said, "Just trying to get my foot in the door. Hope you enjoy these goodies.

I'll give you a call next week to see how I can help. Enjoy, Charlene." The customers loved it, and many became buyers!

Your approach will vary depending on whether you are selling B2B (business to business)—as I was when using the baskets—or B2C (business to consumer). Get creative, to the extent that your budget allows. Send online gift certificates, food, and anything else you can think of to garner attention. If you are selling directly to consumers, use coupons and incentives to inspire their interest. Who doesn't like getting a great deal through a perk or discount? Remember that luxurious massage you booked because you got a tempting offer? Inspire your customers to take similar action by lighting a fire under their butts or giving them something they can't refuse.

Whether or not you make your sales goals often comes down to a numbers game. The more calls (or outreach attempts) you make, the more sales you'll eventually get, and that's the bottom line. Customers will not just appear waving their credit cards at you, so don't expect them to—you'll have to hustle. Start slowly and build from there. Really listen to people and respond appropriately. Follow up by email to thank them for their time that very same day—even if you didn't get the sale. Make a note on your calendar to circle back again in another month or so, if appropriate. The squeaky wheel gets the grease (not the quiet one).

Your Mindset Shift will be complete when you address any apprehensions that you have that may be related to selling. These could come disguised as any number of common fears for women, including the fear of failure, the fear that you are being too pushy, or the fear that you are going to bug or annoy someone. You must recognize that these worries are holding you back in your business and get over them. Remember that anyone is lucky to have you in their day, including your target customers! Make a list of potential objections that you might get before you make that outreach attempt, and develop what your response to each objection will be. You need to be ready in advance so that you know what to say. Role-play before you go into it. Phone a friend for help with this; you can have a lot of fun with it over a glass of wine.

Making Other Attitude Adjustments

So far in this chapter, we've focused on tangible actions you can take to catapult your startup with your new entrepreneurial mindset. But since so much of business success begins with an inside job, I want to share the following tips about how your attitude as a woman business owner can help you achieve your entrepreneurial goals.

Believe in Your Message

Remind yourself that you have a product that is useful and important. Your message is worth being heard. You are not bothering people or sucking up their time. Yes, you are putting yourself out there to grow your business and achieve professional success—*and* you are helping others in the process. Remember your value and don't discount yourself or your products or services. I mentioned before the strategy of thinking of yourself as trying to meet others' needs instead of selling. So, imagine yourself as a match-maker—matching the right product with the right customers. And I bet you're damn good at it! When you are genuine and passionate about what you do, the sales will follow. Stay positive, girl!

Be Candid with Yourself

If you've embraced the entrepreneurial mindset, then celebrate that you are a saleswoman from this day forward. The fact is, your sales history may go back further than you think. Maybe you sold 300 candy bars for a fund-raiser back in the third grade by going door to door, loving the sense of accomplishment that you got when you tallied up your earnings. Well, you are back at it again, in control of how much you sell and how much you ultimately earn. The more outreach you do, the more profit you'll potentially bring in. Isn't it wonderful to have that kind of control over your destiny?

Remember What Mom Said

Many girls learn the most from their moms (or another female role model). Whoever your role model was, you can draw on her advice and influence, as it can have a tremendous impact on your Mindset Shift and ability to succeed as a fempreneur. I'd like to share a few things that I learned from my mom in hopes that they inspire you as well. While I don't remember her offering me loads of business or career advice when I was growing up, there were three sayings that she repeated to me often, and they more than apply to entrepreneurship:

- **"God helps those who help themselves."** At times, I thought Mom was saying this because she was busy and just didn't want to stop what she was doing. But in retrospect, I can see what she was really telling me was to develop the mindset of taking initiative, standing on my own, and not waiting around for other people to make things happen. It worked. Now I never pause waiting for others, particularly as an entrepreneur. I always take the first step and make sure I achieve the goals that I've set for myself. Being self-motivated is what a woman's entrepreneurial journey is all about.

- **"Fight your own battles."** While hearing this as a child could be very frustrating, this saying has also grown on me over time, particularly where entrepreneurship is concerned. Whenever there was a squabble or a problem, I wanted my mom to intervene on my behalf. Instead, I was met with that same phrase. Once more, she was trying to build resilience and get me to resolve my own conflicts and setbacks when they arose. A fempreneur needs to have the ability to handle obstacles and pivot. That I do, and you can too.

- **"You catch more flies with honey than with vinegar."** This has been a big one in my mental toolbox, and a principle that I always try to live by (though it's not always easy). My great-great-grandmother embraced this saying, and continuing to pass it down, I frequently repeat it to my own two girls. It means that being kind is always the best option, even in a tense situation. When you are nice, people are more willing to help you, listen to you, buy from you, or give you what you need. If you are angry or defensive, they will usually become the same and will be much less likely to do what you want. Let's face it—as female entrepreneurs, we need to catch all the flies we can, so lay that honey out there.

FINAL THOUGHTS

You will never gain anything if you don't put yourself and your business front and center. It's going to take a lot of grit and determination, but if you are tenacious and begin to shift your mindset with the steps we've discussed in this chapter—taking the plunge, developing confidence, considering a side hustle, pinpointing your niche and target market, working on your MVP and business plan, selecting funding options, honing your approach to pitching and selling, fine-tuning your attitude, and continuing to build— you'll get there. So, go ahead and flip that switch and kick-start the journey toward launching your inner entrepreneur!

EMBRACING AN ENTREPRENEURIAL ATTITUDE

So, you're ready to join the entrepreneurial pack. Welcome and congratulations. Now it's time to start your second Mindset Shift: embracing an entrepreneurial attitude. There are no instant success stories or quick paths to riches. It's not about who you know or being lucky. You are going to have to work. Envision your favorite fempreneur and chances are she started working in her garage or at the dining room table. There are many of them out there today:

- Nancy Whiteman began her $25 million food business, Wana Brands, in her kitchen.
- Huda Kattan started her eyelash company as a home side hustle when she had a hard time finding quality false eyelashes as a makeup artist and made her minx eyelashes to fill that void.

- Angie Hicks also saw a huge gap in the market and started her now well-known company, Angie's List. This successful startup, which provides consumer reviews for local service providers, began simply as neighbors sharing information with neighbors.
- Tory Burch built her fashion brand and empire after working for several other fashion designers first, starting off designing clothes in her kitchen.
- Jennifer Hyman's company, Rent the Runway, began as a small campus pop-up shop launched to make wearing designer clothing affordable for all women, filling yet another hole in the market.

These names don't even scratch the surface when it comes to women cashing in on entrepreneurial opportunities.

Paying Your Dues and Making Strategic Moves

Now it's your turn to channel your inner entrepreneur. Brace yourself, because you're likely to feel very overwhelmed when you first begin to take on this attitude adjustment. You're probably wondering how refining your outlook as a business owner can help you stand out among your competitors. The answer is that until you believe that you really *are* an entrepreneur and can become a successful one, you may limit yourself in what you achieve—you have to see it first to become it.

With that in mind, some of this is a return to the basics that we discussed in Mindset Shift 1. The best way to proceed is to confidently pinpoint your niche, filling a void, and avoiding the urge to compete only on price. An entrepreneurial attitude also means focusing on serving your clients and serving them well. This is how you'll be able to effectively lure customers away from larger companies. Again, this is back to business fundamentals: providing good customer service that includes really listening to your clients, being as responsive as possible, and making sure that you follow through with what you say you are going to do.

Another part of this second Mindset Shift is being present to serve customers at all levels, not walling yourself up at the top of your company. Personally ensure that the products and services that your team delivers are of extremely high quality, and never let customers receive a product that is less than what you would want for yourself if you were in their shoes. Pull upon your own experience as a consumer and those times when you were disappointed with a product or service, like when a lipstick you were waiting for arrived in the wrong shade and you couldn't get anyone to help you when you called the company for an exchange. How did you feel when you were stuck with *Mango Sunrise* when you really wanted *Screaming Siren*? Make sure that your customers don't experience the same annoyance, work hard to build rapport with them, and always respond quickly to their feedback and ideas. Bigger organizations are not nearly as nimble and can't pivot as quickly as you can in response to your clients. Work steadily and diligently in these directions with an unshakeable entrepreneurial attitude, and your results will build over time.

Getting these two essentials right—pinpointing your niche and providing customers with a high level of quality and service—can be game changing, but these steps are not all that's needed in this Mindset Shift to obtain success as a fempreneur. A recent study found that 90 percent of startups will fail.[1] A lot of this has to do with entrepreneurs who launch businesses but lack the tenacity to see them through. There is a learning curve associated with becoming an entrepreneur, so don't expect overnight results. Surviving year one is typically the most challenging, as around 20 percent of small businesses will fail within their first year, according to the U.S. Bureau of Labor Statistics.[2]

Determining Your Why

As another part of your Mindset Shift—and as an additional method to increase your confidence and persistence—you will also need to know what you want, which requires understanding your *why*. Figuring out your *why* will be central to your forward momentum and every entrepreneurial move that you make. If you don't understand your *why*, your customers won't either. Ask yourself a few important questions:

- Why are you launching this business in the first place?
- What drives you?
- How are you helping your customers, and what do you want to accomplish?
- Why is entrepreneurship the right choice for you?
- Why now? And why this business?

Once you have clear answers to these questions, you'll have what you need to confidently and persistently continue on your path. Knowing your *why* is paramount to formulating your strategic plans and attacking your fempreneurial goals. In the words of Nietzsche, "he who has a *why* can endure any *how*."[3]

Getting Your Game On

Once you've zeroed in on your *why*, it's time to compete (part of your *how*). Success in entrepreneurship is very much like a game—part chess match, part poker tournament, and part schoolyard soccer competition. You've got to make decisive moves in a really strategic way, bluff on occasion when you want others to think that you have a better hand, and pass the ball to and from teammates to hit your goals. Sometimes, it will be a straight line to a quick score, and at other times, you will have to double back, up the ante, and formulate a new plan.

I tackle business in this gamelike manner, face forward, shin guards on straight, while making those calculated moves—my end goals always in sight. This competitive vision is what helps determined fempreneurs persevere after others fold. Having your eye on the prize, like Ruth Fertel, founder of the world-famous restaurant chain Ruth's Chris Steakhouse, is key. She zigged and zagged, changing her game strategy around a couple of times before ultimately achieving success after her initial foray in the restaurant business fell apart.

Tapping into Passion and Grit

In addition to being steadfast and tenacious, there are a number of other attitudinal qualities that are central to getting through that first year in business and beyond, with grit and passion being among the most important. Given the many obstacles that startup founders take on every day, grit is essential.

To succeed long term, entrepreneurs must have a persistent belief that their business will defy the dismal statistics to become a thriving enterprise. An attitude of grit involves working because you believe that the work you are doing is important and worth it, not because you are forced to.

As psychologist and author Angela Duckworth explains, "Grit is sticking with your future day in, day out and not just for the week, not just for the month, but for years."[4] You've got to love what you're doing because you must embrace and go after it with all of your heart in order to get your company off the ground and eventually thriving. That love boils down to passion—that strong feeling of enthusiasm or excitement for something or about doing something.

Fashion designer and founder of her eponymous brand Eileen Fisher famously said, "Life-fulfilling work is never about the money—when you feel true passion for something, you instinctively find ways to nurture it."[5] Passion is an important attitude component for fempreneurs because it can impact how customers, employees, and potential investors see you. A business owner's passion can indicate her confidence in her brand, her ability to overcome setbacks, the type of leader she is, her level of motivation, and how well she will be able to persuade others to buy her offerings. That passion has to be backed by a strong product or service too, of course, in order to establish credibility and trust with her stakeholders.

Becoming Grittier

Passion and grit go hand in hand. Entrepreneurs need the persistent attitude of grit because it can be lonely to be on your own and in charge of a business, which may require failing a lot before you succeed. Grit is critical so that you don't become too overwhelmed and throw in the towel prematurely. The good news is that studies by grit expert Angela Duckworth found women to be grittier than men.[6] However, women must still work to increase their grit to persist as entrepreneurs, as there are numerous studies that suggest that women may be less successful in entrepreneurial endeavors than their male counterparts, and that businesses owned by women often have lower revenue and growth and fail more often than those run by men.[7]

Given these somewhat discouraging findings, grit will be a vital part of your Mindset Shift in order to propel your journey as a fempreneur. It's also important to note that your level of grit is not "fixed," to use Duckworth's terminology, but that with a *growth mindset*, it can be further developed through practice and rebounding from failures. Taking action is often half the battle, as discussed in Mindset Shift 1. Startup leaders don't talk about getting things done; they actually do them.

Duckworth notes that talent counts once and effort counts twice, taking it a step further with an actual equation that she devised:[8]

$$\text{Talent} \times \text{Effort} = \text{Skill}$$

and

$$\text{Skill} \times \text{Effort} = \text{Achievement}$$

In other words, you get grittier through practice, and the more you practice, the more developed you and your skills will become. So give yourself some goals in terms of improvement. Where do you want to be in six months or a year? What do you hope to get better at or learn to do? Thinking through your answers to these types of questions early in your entrepreneurial journey can help you develop an attitude that's based on grit.

Taking Ownership

Do you know any particularly gritty people? It can pay off in improvements to your own attitude if you surround yourself with them. After all, we pick up so much from those we flock with. Having a clear vision and optimistic expectations, as well as giving yourself enough time to meet your goals, also can lead to an increase in grittiness. Your vision—which involves how you see your initial startup in terms of its personal meaning to you, and then how you envision it evolving over time—is what keeps you interested in your business for the long haul.

It's also important to see failure as an opportunity to grow and not be discouraged by it, instead holding on to hope for a better future, based on implementing the lessons from mistakes. In the words of Oprah Winfrey, "Think like a queen. A queen is not afraid to fail."[9] You are the queen of your company. Be certain that you have time to make it happen and to accomplish your goals. If you've set an unrealistic time frame, it can lead to unnecessary disappointment, while mapping out a more realistic schedule of milestones to meet can help you get there step by step. Girl, grab your scepter and get after it!

The key to a gritty attitude is taking responsibility for your own progress and forward momentum. After all, as a startup leader, you're at the helm. Grit involves having the courage and gumption to keep plowing on. It's also aided by showing loyalty, both to yourself and your vision and to your business to see it through challenges. Tory Burch, the executive chairman and chief creative officer of her own mega fashion brand, said, "One of the best pieces of advice I ever received from my parents is to think of negativity as noise. Believe in yourself and what you're doing. Remember: If the most unique ideas were obvious to everyone, there wouldn't be entrepreneurs. The one thing that every entrepreneurial journey has in common is that there are many, many steps on the road to success."[10]

This advice of self-focus applies well when considering your competitors, too. Don't worry too much about what others in your market are doing, outside of having a general sense of trends. Instead, focus on what *you* can control—your startup and the actions you are taking to grow revenue. The famous female entrepreneurs I've mentioned had not only passion for their business, but also a mindset of grit and determination to follow their dreams and achieve success. Look at author and businesswoman Arianna Huffington and her global media empire. She has shown great fortitude while expanding her business domain over the years—and she has her gritty attitude partly to thank for it.

Failing First

Don't expect perfection in the early days, weeks, months, and even initial years of developing your entrepreneurial mindset. Launching a company inherently involves trying new things that don't always pan out—but that's okay and even to be expected. The important thing is to keep evolving from these trials and errors, continuously implementing any new insights that you've absorbed. To state this another way: you and your startup won't improve until you fail at some aspect of it. And keep in mind that it's not so much about the fall itself, but how quickly you can bounce up and try again—which again comes back to your gritty entrepreneurial attitude.

It can be hard to push on when things aren't going well in some aspect of your business, but being tenacious is something that you must focus on every single day despite any setbacks or obstacles. Inevitably, everyone hits snags, both personally and professionally. Shifting your mindset to bring out your grit is vital for times when you experience those tough patches. Whether it's losing a client, bid, or partnership, you need to train your mind to be flexible enough to go forward. As you work on developing this new way of thinking, it can help to remember that entrepreneurship is about continual reinvention and growth; in other words, flopping is part of the gig. Can you own your losses and move ahead? If you can, then your fempreneurial attitude is growing stronger. Any time spent wallowing in regret, sorrow, or self-pity without reflecting on what you learned is wasted. Having an entrepreneurial outlook means recognizing that this is precious time that you could be using to make another deal or come up with a different alternative instead. Own the outcomes, both good and bad, and make the most of every day. As Estée Lauder said, "I never dreamed about success. I worked for it."[11]

Embracing Risk Taking

Becoming comfortable with taking risks is part of this Mindset Shift process. According to recent research, women have just as big of an appetite for taking risks as men; however, many women still resist it to some extent.[12] One of the main reasons that women struggle with risk, according to a KPMG study, is that they are often afraid of how others will perceive them.[13] Michele Meyer-Shipp, KPMG's chief diversity officer, believes that the solution lies in women finding ways to "get comfortable being uncomfortable."[14] As the head of a company, getting comfortable with risk taking is a critical attitude adjustment, as risk leads to innovation, which can help you achieve your startup goals. You might be able to get by with doing things the same way they've always been done in some industries, but for most markets, that is exactly the *wrong* type of mindset, and one that will lead to owning a mediocre business.

As a female entrepreneur, you will have to step outside of your comfort zone repeatedly. It is your job to temper that risk with the proper preparation and research, learning as much as you can about an industry before getting into it, and continuing to stay on top of it while operating in that market. Try things you think you can't do, embrace failure when it happens, and keep trying again as prudent. You will not be able to shy away from putting yourself front and center when you are driving the ship. As Dr. Maya Angelou, author and poet, said, "I love to see a young girl go out and grab the world by the lapels. Life's a bitch. You've got to go out and kick ass."[15] So go kick some ass, girl!

Dealing with Haters

Here's another part of your entrepreneurial attitude adjustment that's needed but can be uncomfortable for some women to think about: not everyone is going to like you. This is especially true as you stand out from the crowd more and more with your business and innovative ideas. As you go out on a limb and try to make a splash in your industry, don't be surprised if you encounter some people or groups who greet you with resistance or envy. These naysayers and haters unfortunately are out there. You can't lose valuable energy and momentum, though, worrying about what others think of you, so you'll need to shift your mindset to effectively deal with haters as well.

A multitude of research has shown that women have more of an emotional reaction to negative stimuli than men.[16] Based on these studies, and recognizing the reality that some people may try to discourage or dissuade you from pursuing your entrepreneurial vision, a critical part of your Mindset Shift must include learning to develop a thicker skin. One way to do this is to recognize that negativity from others often stems from their own insecurities and sometimes even jealousy—it has more to do with them than you. Perhaps they lack the confidence to tackle the type of gutsy new business launch that you are leading, or they're insecure seeing others succeed when they aren't happy with their own career progress. Whatever the case, be prepared for the occasional hater to be out there, sometimes in the form of strangers, and sometimes, even worse, in people who are close to you.

When dealing with this sort of negative energy, don't worry, you won't be alone; every person who has achieved a certain degree of success has had their own gang of haters. Personally, I've found that the best way to deal with the naysayers is to embrace them. There have been times when I've achieved personal milestones (like when I got a promotion, launched a book, or defended my doctoral dissertation) and wanted to shout the news from the rooftops. I thought that all of my acquaintances would be equally happy for me, but I found that wasn't necessarily the case. I quickly learned to approach these haters a little differently, and you should, too.

First, get to the heart of the matter and find out what's making these unpleasant noisemakers resist your business. Listen to what they have to say and respond patiently and respectfully, doing what you can to win them over. It can be difficult to give haters a microphone, but often, they just want to be heard, and if you listen to them, it can help silence their spite. If they're attacking you or your company online, resist the urge to delete their comments or send hate back. Instead, respond professionally by remaining calm and doing what you can to help solve their issue.

If you encounter haters in your own circle and personal life, you may have to reduce or eliminate contact with them—and that's okay. I've had to distance myself a few times when I felt friends sending too much animosity my way. According to Gayle King, television personality and broadcast journalist, "When people don't want the best for you, they are not the best for you."[17] Gayle is right—no matter what you do in business (and in life), you'll never please everyone. If you know that going in as a fempreneur, this insight can help you hang on to your entrepreneurial, gritty mindset, rather than letting the haters of the world derail you.

Despite your best efforts, however, there may be times when you find yourself getting defensive in the face of a hater and need a useful tactic to deal with it. In those instances, try to pause and reflect on what's been said before reacting. It can also be helpful to get some more information, rather than responding with a knee-jerk reaction. When gathering feedback, work to stay present in the moment. Remain conscious of any bias you might have going in, be sure to separate facts from feelings, and establish cue words or phrases to help you refocus and stop your defensiveness. As leadership guru Ken Blanchard said, "Feedback is the breakfast of champions."[18] Look at feedback from haters like a tall glass of orange juice that, once swallowed, will make you stronger.

While it sucks in many ways to have to deal with negative people who don't support your business goals, there's a bright side to it: having haters can be an indication that you're making big moves and getting close to the success you've been craving. You will hit your largest setback, or greatest resistance, just before you get your biggest breakthrough. So many famous entrepreneurs were on the verge of giving up just before they hit it big. Realize that opposition comes with the territory of success, and don't take it personally. The best way to deal with a hater is to not hate back, but to try to communicate with them and hear their complaint. Although it won't always make a difference, you just may be surprised at the way they respond to your positive example. In the words of Taylor Swift, award-winning singer and songwriter, learn to "shake it off, shake it off."

Closing the Confidence Gap

Having the ability to stand up to your detractors also relates to your confidence—another critical component of this second Mindset Shift. You will need faith in spades to become a thriving startup mogul, and women tend to have more difficulty owning their successes, according to research involving female entrepreneurs.[19]

The opposite of confidence is fear, which is something that customers can sense—and it will make them afraid to do business with you. You must radiate an attitude of assurance, or your target market will not completely trust you. If they are not confident in you, you will lose the sale (egads!). Always respond to a customer's questions with poise and conviction, even if you have to scramble to do what they request. Just perform your research and make it happen for them. If it's a reasonable ask, the answer should always be affirmative. As pop star Katy Perry says, "If you're presenting yourself with confidence, you can pull off pretty much anything."[20]

Self-confidence doesn't come easily for most women, but you must have it as a startup leader. For their book *The Confidence Code,* researchers Katty Kay and Claire Shipman surveyed thousands of women and discovered that there was a "confidence gap" between men and women that caused career limitation and frustration for women. Closing this gap will be necessary to the longevity of your entrepreneurial venture, which is why this Mindset Shift is so pivotal to your journey as a female business owner.

Validating some of the other research mentioned in this chapter, Kay and Shipman also found that "women worry more about being disliked, appearing unattractive, outshining others or grabbing too much attention."[21] There is medical science to back up these findings. Louann Brizendine, a neuropsychiatrist at the University California, San Francisco, states that "it turns out there's an area of your brain that's assigned the task of negative thinking. It's judgmental. It says, 'I'm too fat' or 'I'm too old.' It's a barometer of every social interaction you have. It goes on red alert when the feedback you're getting from other people isn't going well."[22] Worse yet, this part of the brain is the anterior cingulate cortex, which is involved in certain higher-level functions like emotion, and it's actually larger and more influential in some women.

Many professionals believe that men are almost always more confident than women, even when the women are equally or more talented, and, unfortunately, confidence was discovered to be more important than competence when it comes to business success, according to some *Harvard Business Review* research.[23] To further drive home this point, there is a well-known study that was conducted by McKinsey at Hewlett-Packard that showed men applied for promotions when they met 60 percent of the qualifications that were required, whereas women applied only when they met 100 percent of those same qualifications.[24] That study underscored the fact that women are wired to feel confident only when they are perfect or close to it.

When you are just starting out in business, you will be far from perfect—so you'll need to do what you can to infuse a confident mindset into your attitude toolbox. Sheryl Sandberg, chief operating officer of Facebook, said, "Trying to do it all and expecting it all can be done exactly right is a recipe for disappointment. Perfection is the enemy."[25] Resist the urge to wait on that elusive perfection. As we saw in Mindset Shift 1, becoming a successful business owner hinges on taking action—which may never happen if you let perfectionism get the better of you. So, do the work to shift your mindset away from flawlessness and toward execution.

Developing Persistence

Your attitude adjustment related to confidence is not over once you make your first sale either, as you've got to keep going and make additional sales. Assume that you'll have repeat business (even before you do) and think of customers in terms of long-term relationships. This is where tenacity and persistence—cousins of grit—are crucial. Tenacity is "the quality of being determined," and persistence is the "obstinate continuance in a course of action in spite of difficulty or opposition."[26]

If you need help developing an attitude conducive to these traits, why not create a mastermind group—which is a peer-to-peer mentoring group—with a few other startup leaders to swap advice and encourage one another? The concept of a mastermind group is not new. It was first introduced in 1925 in Napoleon Hill's book *The Law of Success*. In this type of cooperative clique, you can lean on one another and hold each other accountable to goals, supporting all group members' successes and failures. I'm a member of a female mastermind group, and I love it. It's encouraging to interact with the other women, and our collaboration gives us all a big boost in terms of cultivating an attitude of persistence.

Believing in Yourself

Based on the research I mentioned that shows women struggle more than men with confidence issues, you are going to have to keep the goal of growing your confidence top of mind. This part of the entrepreneurial attitude shift involves learning to truly believe in yourself, which isn't a one-and-done process. I'll be the first to admit that this can be particularly challenging, so it's important to take baby steps over time to bolster your self-esteem. One idea that has worked for me and the women business owners who I mentor is to go old school: use a pen and paper to make a list of those things you like most about yourself; then ask others to contribute their observations of your strengths. Do you write a mean business proposal, have a smile that can outshine the sun, or know the ins and outs of your industry much better than most? Whatever amazing assets are on your list, hang it somewhere as a reminder for those days when your self-esteem wanes. This technique can offer an instant mood boost, which goes a long way toward attitude. You can even take it a step further and create an actual brag sheet of all your accomplishments, skills, and traits (for internal use only). I'm sure you've heard the term *stroking the male ego*. This time, ladies, it's time to stroke yours.

As part of bolstering self-esteem, avoid the urge to be too hard on yourself. One way that you can accomplish this is to build your fact-finding or probing skills, and when you feel self-doubt creeping in, leverage them more effectively. For example, if something goes wrong or happens that you don't understand with a client or business associate, ask questions and seek clarification and feedback. Having the real scoop can provide the context you need to avoid unnecessary self-blame. As detailed in the "haters" section, if you receive criticism, remain calm and try not to get defensive.

Another step that can help you to increase your belief and conviction in yourself and your business is to endeavor to always address others in a way that encourages them. When you help people, you are also helping to boost your confidence. Always speak with the end goal of being able to inspire, as people are typically moved by emotion, the speaker's status, or intellectual reasoning. Figure out what motivates each person and then tailor your message to them accordingly. As you fine-tune your conversational skills, your self-esteem and influence will expand. Choose your words with care and frame them so that they will have the highest impact on your audience, supporting their comments and thereby building trust with them. This support works by asking deep questions and using encouraging phrases like "I understand" or "I hear what you're saying," or by repeating a message back. Listen, be present, and pay attention to your body language too. You will continue to build influence, begin to stand a little taller, and deliver your messages with a stronger belief in yourself.

Increasing Patience

As your faith in your abilities builds, it's also critical to learn to be patient and get comfortable with the fact that good things rarely happen overnight. That's why developing patience is another key component of your Mindset Shift. Most things worth achieving involve a lot of work, and often a long wait. Understand that before you begin, and increase your inner resolve knowing that you have what it takes to accomplish your goals. People often ask me how they can do what I'm doing, or how I got involved with some of the projects that I have. I feel as if they often want some secret recipe or quick path that they can trace—but there isn't one. I have simply been working hard to identify opportunities and achieve my goals. There has been no shortcut or straight line for me. The more I've put in, the more I've taken out, and each path is unique. As I always explain, you can never follow exactly what someone else did and expect it to work. You have to find your own route, leaning heavily on your confidence, trial and error, patience and persistence. It's about 90 percent hard work and 10 percent timing and luck.

Finding the Silver Lining

Your Mindset Shift will remain incomplete if you don't develop the ability to see the silver lining in every situation. This requires training yourself to find the good even when you're hit with something bad. You can do so by looking at barriers as opportunities to improve and by removing negative words—such as *don't, can't, shouldn't, fail*, and *no*—from your vocabulary. Sound impossible? I promise, it's not. Keeping your internal talk upbeat despite the initial disappointment and unearthing a way to uncover the positive will help you find your silver lining.

Another way you can start to fight your natural tendency toward negativity is to reflect on the ways you have dealt with similar situations in the past, then apply those lessons to your current scenario. This time, approach it from a 100-foot perspective and let go of what you can't change while coming up with a strategy for what you can do to move forward in a more positive way—one that is better for you. For example, perhaps you were furloughed and now have the opportunity to change your career direction, just like you always dreamed about. That's the bright spot (and it's a big one) in a negative situation. I once had a supervisor give me a low annual merit increase despite being told by others that I was a top performer. Clearly, I was not being valued by this supervisor, and the lack of a larger merit increase actually turned out to be just the push I needed to move on. I was in the wrong place, and as a result of this negative event, I determined that I could do better on my own as a fempreneur (the bright side). Listen to what your environment is telling you and let discouraging events push you toward more positive ones. Adjust your perspective and uncover the silver lining!

Getting Unstuck

At times when you feel like you can't see anything positive about a situation, the answer is often to tap into outside sources of energy. Even if you aren't able to connect with someone in person for a mood boost, think about ways to channel energy from sources that lift you—maybe calling a friend, hitting the treadmill, or scheduling a Zoom meeting with your mastermind group. Figure out what external hits will motivate you to bring back an optimistic outlook. For me, there's nothing like kayaking or taking a walk outdoors to restore my happiness and ability to be enthusiastic. I call my friends a lot too (thanks for the mood boosts, ladies).

Your positive entrepreneurial attitude should also incorporate celebrating failures as well as successes—while one is definitely more fun than the other, they are both important turning points for a business owner—and always have a plan B (C, D, E, and F too). These backups should be a built-in part of your strategic formulation. Finally, in your quest to keep your mind focused on the silver lining, find yourself an ups-and-downs buddy: someone who will cheer you up no matter what. This might be a member of your entrepreneurial posse, a significant other, or a good friend who always makes you laugh. As Mary Kay Ash, iconic founder of Mary Kay Cosmetics, said, "Don't limit yourself. Many people limit themselves to what they think they can do. You can go as far as your mind lets you. What you believe, remember, you can achieve."[27]

Overcoming Impostor Syndrome

The concept of "impostor syndrome" was first introduced as the idea that some successful women feel they don't really belong, have only gotten lucky, or haven't really earned their successes.[28] It has since been determined that both men and women suffer from imposter syndrome. In fact, it's estimated that 70 percent of people feel like an impostor at some point or another in their lives, although it's more common for women and minorities.[29] One critical area where many women suffer from impostor syndrome is in business, no matter their profession. For example, a bestselling female author said "[even] after publishing her 11th book, that every time she wrote another one, she'd think to herself: 'Uh-oh, they're going to find out now. I've run a game on everybody."[30]

It's extremely common for women to feel this way and doubt their achievements even after enormous success. Worse yet, impostor syndrome can be more prevalent for those embarking on a new endeavor, which you will be doing as a budding business owner. As a female founder, it is crucial for you to overcome this feeling as part of this second Mindset Shift.

The impostor phenomenon boils down to your own damaging self-talk and your responses to feelings of inadequacy. It can stem from an overemphasis on achievement in your family growing up, your personality, and other psychological influences like anxiety and neuroticism.[31] According to impostor syndrome expert Valerie Young, there are several different types of behavior patterns, or archetypes, that women act out in relation to their defensive response to impostor syndrome. These archetypes include:

- The perfectionist: a woman who sets impossibly high standards for herself
- The superwoman: someone who works extremely hard to prove that she is not an impostor

- The expert: someone who must know everything possible before she begins a project where she doesn't feel completely comfortable
- The soloist: someone who doesn't like to ask for help for fear of looking like a failure
- The natural genius: someone who equates struggle or hard work with inadequacy[32]

If you're dealing with impostor syndrome and feel it moving your entrepreneurial attitude in the wrong direction, the first step is to know that everyone feels inadequate at times (myself included). Learn to understand that these feelings are just feelings, not the truth about you. Acknowledge your thoughts and look at them from a different angle by putting some distance between yourself and the thought. Don't let it sink in—detach from it and debate it. What you say to yourself is how you will see yourself, so you should consistently try to turn negativity around. Implement ways to recognize when you are out of your comfort zone and when you feel perfectly capable. Embrace both instances, reminding yourself that you shouldn't always know the answer—no one does.

It can also be useful to tell yourself how adequate and amazing you actually are. Give yourself a pep talk and instructions if you feel like an impostor: "Mary, you've got this," or "Charlotte, you are awesome!" Never, ever, ever, write off anything you've achieved as merely being lucky. You are not lucky: you are hard-working and capable. Don't ever question it.

When going into a situation where you are feeling a little insecure, visualize yourself landing the deal, delivering a killer presentation, or just plain kicking ass. When you think about it positively and actually see yourself succeeding, you will feel less like a fraud and perform better too. It's also a wise strategy to remind yourself that no one is flawless, and that you do have a high level of expertise—yes, you!

Always stretch yourself and look for methods to enhance your skills and knowledge when there is a gap. Many times, I've been in professional situations where I thought I was in over my head but kept swimming anyhow, rising to those occasions. Although it may sound simplistic, telling yourself the truth—that you are *not* an impostor, and that you belong alongside the other entrepreneurs in your industry—can help you continue to develop your entrepreneurial mindset rather than letting impostor syndrome stop you.

Fighting Self-Sabotage

Self-sabotage, the evil stepsister of impostor syndrome, occurs when your pessimistic internal dialogue hijacks your brain and you end up talking yourself out of positive things. Have you ever talked yourself out of a promotion or interesting business opportunity? Told yourself you couldn't do it or weren't good enough? Self-sabotage might result in having a negative viewpoint about your abilities or self-worth, which can hinder your mood and, ultimately, your performance (and the success of your business). Don't tell yourself these lies.

Research shows that women sabotage their goals for many reasons, including fear, low self-esteem, and as a form of self-preservation or protection. Leslie Feinzaig, CEO of the Female Founders Alliance, identified three main forms of self-sabotage in female founders, which are encapsulated in these statements: "My needs come last," "I'm not good enough," and "I'm not ready."[33] Pay attention to whether these types of toxic mindsets are controlling your thought processes and work *hard* to eliminate them from your life. Some signs of self-sabotage include:

- An inability to recover from difficulties
- Telling yourself that you can't do something, or that you're not talented or competent
- Freezing in critical business situations
- Having poor working relationships and/or being unable to achieve goals
- Talking yourself out of positive steps forward

If any of those signs resonate with you, here are some of my top tips to thwart self-sabotage:

- Change your mindset by keeping a daily journal outlining all of the good things happening in your business (and life).
- Discuss your feelings with someone who can help, whether a personal friend, career coach, or professional therapist.
- Set goals for yourself and break them down into the steps that you'll take to achieve them.
- Practice self-care by getting enough sleep, establishing a fitness routine, and eating well.

- Create a mantra about your value and self-worth to repeat when feelings of self-sabotage or negative internal dialogue creep in.
- Engage in activities that boost your esteem and reenergize you.
- Be your own best friend and do what you can to pull yourself up.
- Tell yourself that you are good enough!
- Tell yourself that your needs come first!
- Tell yourself that you are ready for all the great things that are waiting for you and all the success and prosperity that you deserve!

In the words of Arianna Huffington: "We need to accept that we won't always make the right decisions, that we'll screw up royally sometimes—understanding that failure is not the opposite of success, it's part of success."[34]

FINAL THOUGHTS

Entrepreneurial Mindset Shift 2 is huge and will fuel you for the rest of the Mindset Shifts still to come. Remember the strategies we've discussed in this chapter: paying your dues, making strategic moves, determining your why, getting your game on, tapping into passion and grit, taking ownership, and embracing risk-taking and failure. You have also learned to become more adept at dealing with haters, closing the confidence gap, developing persistence and self-belief, increasing patience and the ability to get unstuck, and overcoming impostor syndrome and self-sabotage. Make all of these strategies a part of your everyday mindset and use them to fuel your entrepreneurial fire! Girl, go out there and make it happen with confidence, grit, perseverance, and all the passion you can muster—you are not only worth it, you've earned it!

CULTIVATING FINANCIAL CONFIDENCE

Y ou're becoming more self-assured and have begun to formulate the plans to get your startup going. Pause and celebrate this momentum! You are stretching and growing, but it doesn't end there, which brings us to our third Mindset Shift: cultivating financial confidence.

Money, moolah, cheddar, Benjamins, bacon, dough, coin, or whatever you want to call it is the driving factor for every business owner, and as a new fempreneur, you must start to shift your money mindset. Revenue generation and growth will be critical to the success of your company, so how you think about finances will be vital to fueling that growth and potential profit. Marc Pearlman, *Money Mindset* podcaster and financial advisor, said, "Entrepreneurs who look at the viability of a business's potential to make money without first understanding their own money beliefs are potentially setting themselves up for failure. Since money is the fuel that drives every business, people's money beliefs, for better or worse, are going to reveal themselves within every business structure."[1]

This may be more critical for women. Researcher Laura Huang found that "for female entrepreneurs, the numbers are clear: they own 38% of all businesses in the United States, yet they only receive 2% of all venture financing. And even when they are able to raise money, female entrepreneurs find that it is in amounts much lower than their male counterparts."[2] Because female founders struggle more with raising capital than men do, it makes sense that women may doubt themselves in money matters and have greater challenges than men when it comes to adjusting their money mindset.

Katherine M. Dean, a certified financial planner explains, "In many ways, the financial deck is stacked against women—but that doesn't mean they can't achieve abundance and financial success. It's easy to lose confidence in the face of all these obstacles but breaking through them really comes down to one critical detail: your money mindset."[3] To cultivate your financial confidence, and improve your money mindset, we'll get into tactics related to first understanding and then mastering psychological influences related to money, examining your current finances, budgeting and cutting costs, utilizing bootstrapping, analyzing how your personal finances can impact your business, and delving into methods to improve your negotiation skills. Sound good? Well then, grab your purse, and let's get going!

Understanding Your Psychological Influences

Women's views on financial matters vary depending on a number of psychological influences associated with money, such as their upbringing and past financial history. As the head of your startup, you will need to explore these potential money blocks and address how to recognize and deal with them, paving the way for financial success in business. This is the first part of this third entrepreneurial Mindset Shift.

Perhaps you don't view yourself as someone who's great with finances, or maybe your parents told you that money was the root of all evil. I remember getting scolded once for throwing away a dollar bill that was ripped. I can picture it clearly. I was called over to the garbage can in our kitchen and lectured by both of my parents, who taped the dollar bill back together.

Scenarios like these may have contributed to your own personal blocks. Maybe there wasn't enough money in your family when you were young, or maybe you noticed a lot of frivolous spending and didn't like it. Perhaps you've had to file for bankruptcy or have had times when you were bogged down with a lot of credit card debt. It's okay, it happens. Forgive yourself and put the past in the past. Your entrepreneurial endeavor is a new beginning. If you want to get better with money, you are going to have to address and overcome these blocks. As T. Harv Eker, author of *Secrets of the Millionaire Mind*, says, cultivating a money mindset is often about unlearning. He claims that "it is essential that you recognize your old ways of thinking and acting and how they have gotten you exactly where you are right now"—and unlearn them.[4]

Money Fears

You can begin this unlearning by first looking into and understanding your fears about money. According to one study, one of the biggest fears for women is "always living paycheck to paycheck"; that same research found that they are also more likely to worry about their financial future than men.[5] Have you been experiencing similar worries and finding yourself nervous about your financial outlook? If you're living paycheck to paycheck, there are some ways that you can get beyond it and eradicate that fear.

Financial expert Dave Ramsey suggests paying for your four walls first: your food, shelter, utilities, and transportation.[6] After that, you can spend on other things if there is money left over. He also recommends getting rid of debt as quickly as you can and getting extra cash by selling all the stuff that you have and aren't using (old sporting equipment, clothes, furniture, books, etc.). Unload those dusty rollerblades and that exercise equipment that you only used once (it's okay, I won't tell anyone). When you've stopped living paycheck to paycheck, you'll be able to focus more on your future (and business), which is what you want as part of this money Mindset Shift.

"Women face a unique set of financial challenges that often differ, significantly, from men," says Kerry Hannon of Merrill Lynch.[7] These challenges include being too busy to find time for dealing with investments as well as being paid less than their male counterparts, which often results in having smaller financial nest eggs. Another study found that women's confidence lags around money, with only 27 percent of women believing that they will achieve their goals in terms of financial wealth.[8]

Money Taboos

Another contributing factor is that for women, money has long been a taboo topic—something that we were taught not to discuss. A recent Age Wave study found "61% of women would rather talk about their own death than about money."[9] Doesn't that really say something—preferring to converse about final resting places over finances? That same research found that only 1% of literature in women's magazines is about personal finances, making it glaringly obvious that the media aimed at women has not done much to help. If we are to be financially successful as fempreneurs, we must become more comfortable with the topic of money in order to grow our mastery and maximize our finances.

Building Confidence

When it comes to money, confidence is important. In her book *Women and Money*, Suze Orman unpacks why it is that women, who are so competent in all other areas of their lives, cannot find the same competence when it comes to money.[10] Orman summed up the situation by stating that women have a complicated, dysfunctional relationship with money. That financial competence is exactly what you as a business owner will need to grasp, and it is central to this Mindset Shift.

Mastering Your Psychological Influences

It's not all bad news, though. Women do view money as a way to finance the lifestyle they want to live and to take care of the people that they care about, according to that same Age Wave study, with 77 percent of women seeing money in terms of what it's able to do for their families. So, with that said, it's time to start making this mindset adjustment. Here's how.

Teach Yourself to Love Money

For starters, learn to adore money. Wealth is good—it's just a question of using it the right way. You have the ambition and drive, and you're not lazy, so give yourself permission to make lots of cash. And don't ever feel guilty about your financial success. You've earned it and can even use some of it to have a positive impact on the world. When you're prosperous, you'll be able to take care of yourself and your family and give to charities and nonprofits—all of which are good things. Pull on that confidence we were just talking about as part of this Mindset Shift; know that you have been working hard and deserve to have wealth and be successful. Don't tell yourself otherwise.

Talk About Money

It's also okay, and even critical, to talk about money. We are often taught from a young age that speaking up is unladylike, especially when it comes to money. Yet, you have to speak up and converse about it or no one will know what you're thinking. So, ask a lot of questions and get active in the conversations about your financial future, because it's *your* future! Forget what you've been taught. Train yourself to be more relaxed when discussing finances. You'll need this skill when selling, making deals, and negotiating with suppliers. Back in my sales days, I had a client who always said, "If you don't ask, you don't get." Exactly. You won't get anything if you're not able to voice it.

Practice Financial Transparency

Become more at ease with being transparent about your finances. If you can't afford to take a lavish trip with your friends, be honest with them and tell them that it is not within your budget. Do not give in to peer pressure and spend irresponsibly. In fact, don't feel that you have to do anything—especially something you can't afford—to maintain pretenses or keep up with others in your circle. Doing so would be economically irresponsible, and you are shifting away from that way of thinking as a smart, financially savvy fempreneur!

Lose Financial Baggage

While you're at it, stop using unflattering adjectives to describe your financial situation, such as "poor," "snobby," or "irresponsible." I know that I certainly had some mental baggage in terms of how I saw my monetary status. As part of this Mindset Shift, remove these disparaging words from your identity and vocabulary.

Examining Your Current Finances

Scrutinize your current financial situation from a mindset perspective, then develop strategies related to goal setting and developing monetary targets. You must also become well versed in conducting a spending analysis and improving bad habits related to money management. Beginning with your own personal budget will lessen your stress and also help you better manage the finances when it comes to your startup.

As part of your personal analysis, review and make a list of all of your spending and expenses. Sort them and figure out which of them are necessary and which are not. Do you really need to buy yourself a new pair of shoes every month? (I totally get it, but can you cut it?) Next, look at your income—all sources. Are you spending more than you make? What changes can you implement to have a more positive financial outcome? What do your savings and investment accounts look like? What other debt do you have? What do you want to change there (if anything)?

After that, develop some financial targets and goals. What matters most to you? What do you want to improve or accomplish after reviewing your spending and monetary situation? Do you want to boost your savings? You should have enough to support yourself for about six months to a year. How about paying off some credit card debt or other obligations? Do you want to save some cash in an emergency fund or buy a house or car? Once you've answered these questions, create some SMART (specific, measurable, attainable, realistic, and time-based) goals to ensure that you achieve your targets. For example, it could be that you save $100 every month, or pay off $200 in credit card debt every other week. Try to live below your means and start saving, if you're not already, for retirement and otherwise. You should also check on your credit score, track it, and try to improve it. Give yourself a little goal here too: challenge yourself to a higher number and then reward yourself in a big way when you get there.

As part of this process, set both short- and long-term goals related to your finances. Where do you want to be in six months? One year? Five years? Ten years? I had to do this very same thing for myself when I first jumped into entrepreneurship. I saved up enough to supplement my regular salary for a year. It won't happen if you don't plan for it. Goal setting, as we've discussed and will get further into in the next chapter, is critical to your money Mindset Shift. Set fiscal targets for yourself and keep them.

Even if you feel strapped for cash right now, you will have to change your mindset to see an abundance, particularly when one doesn't exist. Have you heard of the Law of Attraction—the ability to attract what you are focusing on? It applies to your finances too. Situations change quickly, so don't live as if you are broke when you aren't. You'll find a way to pay for some splurges here and there, so indulge from time to time (ensuring they are within your budget, of course) and you'll actually attract more money. Learn to associate money with happiness and meditate about it as well. As part of this Mindset Shift, you should also come up with a money mantra to write or repeat to yourself regularly such as "Every day, I will attract money" or "Money is great and I deserve more." Repeating this mantra will help you reshape the way that you think about and react to money.

Budgeting and Cutting Costs

As a female business owner, how you approach budgeting is also a crucial part of your Mindset Shift. Just like in your personal life, you'll have to create a business budget that you can stick to by paying attention to not only what you have coming in (sales and revenue), but also what's going out. Part of this involves scrutinizing ways to cut costs by identifying unnecessary expenses and inefficiencies that can be reduced or eliminated. Negotiation in the context of cost reduction through suppliers and contractors will also come into play. We'll delve into a number of best practices related to these three areas (budgeting, cutting costs, and negotiation) that you can use for your startup.

Begin by tracking your thoughts related to business expenses. Analyze why you are spending, what your motives are, and if it's necessary. Look for patterns and habits and eliminate destructive behavior. Put yourself in check and commit to capturing your spending activities for a day or two, or even an entire week. By scrutinizing them carefully, you'll uncover what you need to change. Work on enforcing good habits and set a time to look over your payments each week, because you can't improve if you're not aware.

Budgeting is a crucial part of this process, and, as an entrepreneur, you are typically the sole person in charge of the budget at your startup. Remember that in business, you must always be very aware of your bottom line in order to remain profitable. Your bottom line, or profits, are what's left over after subtracting expenses from your revenue. Be mindful that profitability is what investors want to hear about, and the more profitable you are, the happier they'll be. And so will you as the business owner. As such, budgeting effectively is an important component of this Mindset Shift.

When you have your company up and running, carefully analyze what you're spending at your startup, just as you did with your personal expenditures. Approach it with the idea that every one of your current expenses can be reduced or eliminated. You just need to get creative with how you'll do that. Be on the lookout for things that are inefficient, and if what you're spending doesn't add to your profits, you should try to eliminate it. Why pay someone a lot of money to create a website when you can set up your own without much effort? Do you need to have lavish furniture or expensive gadgets? Cut costs first and ask questions later to determine whether or not an expense was necessary.

Give yourself a tough budget, particularly when you're close to launch, and make sure that your employees (if you have any) know that there will be no wiggle room for them. If you do have a team, try to get them on board with the idea of profit maximization by making them come to you for approvals and treating every expense as if it were a major one ($5 or $5,000, it doesn't matter). Be aware that things cost less at certain times, so try to shop during the bargain periods. Make finding less expensive ways to get things done a central part of your culture, and reward money-saving efforts when you see them.

Negotiate with suppliers and contractors too. This is a wonderful way to start reducing costs. Don't accept the first price offered to you. Instead, have a counteroffer ready and shop around to make suppliers bid for your business. Getting your vendors to charge less is much easier than getting your customers to pay more, and it can have a big impact on your profitability. You can even have someone other than the purchaser do the negotiation, because it's likely that the purchaser has developed a personal relationship with the seller. That could mean they won't be as tough on prices. I saw this happen frequently when I was a sales associate. Shoot for lower prices as often as you can. Realize that it's even easier to negotiate with services, as there is more flexibility there, and find out what your competitors are paying too. Maybe they are already buying what you need for less and you can take advantage of the negotiating that they've done previously. It's also a good idea to look at your electronics. You likely don't need so many bells and whistles to get your work done—for example, multiple devices and touchscreen capabilities. Profitability is much, much more important than having fancy equipment.

Other ways to save money in business include reducing travel costs, being frugal with furnishings and décor, reducing office supplies and equipment, cutting down on office space or moving to a home office, holding your meetings virtually or on-site rather than at a hotel or other venue, and so much more. We've so often heard the phrase that "you have to spend money in order to make money." However true that may be, you don't have to go overboard. Analyze all of your costs critically and endeavor to do as much as you can with the lowest spending possible as an element of this part of your Mindset Shift.

Bootstrapping

The willingness to start out by growing your business on a shoestring budget is another indicator of an entrepreneurial mindset and a shift in thinking that you'll need to make. As a woman entrepreneur, you must figure out how to do more with less, analyze your spending in terms of necessity, and explore creative options such as trading for required items, leasing equipment instead of buying it, and purchasing used items. It sounds a bit painful, I'm sure, but I assure you that you can do it.

This brings us to bootstrapping. If you're not familiar with the term, *bootstrapping* is growing your company on this type of limited budget. For starters, don't delay launching your business (even if only as a side hustle) because that will delay bringing money in. You want to focus all of your initial efforts on those things that will generate revenue. Second, only buy what you need immediately and postpone everything else. Always think of your spending in terms of wants versus needs, sticking only with what you need. There is always a way to get more done with less, you just have to get imaginative. Sometimes you can trade equity or services for required items—for example, trade your services for having brochures printed. Instead of buying, lease whenever you can, and purchase used items as they'll be a lot more affordable. Utilize everything that you have before acquiring more. You can also look at franchising, licensing, and joint ventures to maximize profitability.

Addressing Personal Finances

When fine-tuning your money mindset, include a focus on your personal finances as well as those related to your company. As a new fempreneur, you should reduce your personal cost of living (as we've discussed) while getting your startup going and endeavor to live a more minimalistic lifestyle. Declutter and eliminate those things that you don't need; for every item that comes in, throw something out. It feels good to get rid of all those old clothes and items that you no longer use or wear. Good-bye neon cropped top and broken phone charger! This purging practice will help streamline things and prevent you from excessively spending—both at home and at your business.

You must also create a budget for your personal life (in addition to the one you will develop for your company) as part of this process. Make sure that you include things in your personal budget that make you happy. It's been said that around half of your earnings should go to your necessities such as food, housing, transportation, and health care. Allocate around 30 percent to those things you want but aren't necessary and 20 percent to either paying off debt or saving.

As you can see, you will need to make a number of mindset changes when it comes to dealing with finances: modifications in the way that you view money, make purchases, and budget. Embrace this aspect of your Mindset Shift, because it will determine your entrepreneurial bottom line, which you'll be maximizing now!

Negotiation and Raising Capital

Besides those challenges already mentioned, female entrepreneurs face additional barriers, including misperceptions regarding market opportunities, access to traditional networks, underfunding, and managing expansion.[11] Furthermore, access to traditional networks and networking abilities are often cited as some of the main reasons behind gender earnings gaps, according to research by Friederike Mengel.[12] Additionally, women are less likely to negotiate than men—in fact, men initiate negotiations about four times as often as women—as found in studies from Tel Aviv University and the Harvard Kennedy School.[13] These negotiation skills, however, are vital for women in business because they must negotiate with customers and suppliers, as well as when entering into contracts and trying to gain investors.

Facebook chief operating officer Sheryl Sandberg said in a recent forum that women negotiate less often and with less intensity than men.[14] I concur and have seen this repeatedly. Sandberg gave some excellent suggestions to women regarding how to improve their negotiation skills, including trying to be nonthreatening by combining assertive messages with friendly ones, which aim to build relationships while still establishing that you are not a pushover; showing how the deal will benefit all parties instead of just yourself; and solid planning by clearly outlining your must-haves and negotiables and determining what might be important to the other party in advance so that you can leverage it.

I've found these tactics very useful as well. Throughout the years, I've noticed that the greater the level of rapport and the more mutually beneficial the terms, the better the deal. Research has also found that the party who makes the first offer tends to lead the discussion and often ends up with the better arrangement at the end as they are putting what they want out there as a starting point instead of the other way around.[15] It can also be advantageous to bring multiple proposals to the table (this affords you more opportunities to agree) and give yourself room to concede (by knowing what you're willing to trade and budge on, and what you want in return) so that you are able to negotiate more effectively.

When getting ready for a negotiation, you can arm yourself by preparing well so that you are not taken advantage of, anticipating potential negotiation barriers, and crafting your defense beforehand. This will lend you the ammunition you'll need during the negotiation. It can also really help to practice your deal-making skills and look for areas to improve your performance. Role-playing with a friend or practicing in your mastermind group can benefit you in this regard. Overall, you should listen more and talk less when negotiating. If you keep your ears open, you will find out what is most important to the other party, thus revealing areas of opportunity. Perhaps they are willing to budge in one area and not another. You can structure your offer or counteroffer accordingly. Also be willing to give something (a small concession) in order to get something that you really want.

Although your goal is to walk away from the discussion with a deal, don't make a bad deal just for the sake of making a deal. Be sure the agreement you enter into is beneficial to your business. Also, endeavor to study your opponent and realize that they might be using harsh tactics, lying, or extreme bullying demands to get their way. Don't fall for any of these tricks and try not to get overly hung up on small issues. When you have gotten the terms you want, attempt to get the deal done as quickly as possible to avoid having it fall through. Remember, speed is your friend in this regard.

In the end, focus on being unemotional, courteous, and professional, and don't let your ego get in the way of making a solid agreement. Lastly, having several options for making a deal a reality will lessen your anxiety. Try to set yourself up with multiple opportunities so that you don't make any deals out of desperation.

Raising Capital

Getting investors and securing financing have been found to be more difficult for women, so this area too will be critical to your Mindset Shift. A JP Morgan Chase study revealed that female small business owners are "well-represented among businesses that grow organically, but underrepresented among businesses with external financing."[16] And, according to Experian Financial, unequal access to funding and obtaining venture capital were some of the biggest roadblocks for female founders. Experian also stated that "the U.S. Senate Committee on Small Business and Entrepreneurship reported that women receive only 16% of all conventional small business loans" and that when women do apply for loans, they apply for smaller amounts for fear they will be denied.[17] Therefore, when it comes to seeking capital for their companies, fempreneurs also need to make a Mindset Shift in this regard, erasing their apprehension and going after the money needed to grow their business. So grab that moolah!

One way to look for venture capital as a fempreneur is to turn toward female investors and angels (individuals who invest their own money in a new business). More and more of this type of investment group catering to women are popping up all the time. Some examples include 37 Angels, 500 Women, Belle Capital, Broadway Angels, GlobalInvestHer, and Global Fund for Women, to name a few. These groups often focus on investment opportunities and education for female business owners and are typically led by women.

Women can also look for accelerators and incubators to join. Accelerators and incubators are cohort-based programs that provide a number of services, including access to mentors, networking, funding, and sometimes even workspace. They are typically six months to a year and a half long and often provide their services in exchange for some equity in the participant's startup. An accelerator is usually shorter in duration (around six months) than an incubator (around one to two years). The aim of an accelerator is to grow the company as quickly as possible, whereas an incubator is more about nurturing a business at its own pace. Incubators are less likely to invest and take equity in the company compared to accelerators, where that is the more common arrangement.

You will also find a number of grants out there specifically for women entrepreneurs. These include the FedEx Small Business Grant, the Eileen Fisher Women Owned Grant Program, the Halstead Grant, the Open Meadows Foundation Grant, the Cartier Women's Initiative, the Amber Grant, the #GirlBoss Foundation Grant, and more. In addition, the SBA has many grants available for business owners, as mentioned previously. When it comes to grants, you'll have to follow the instructions for application and, if selected, can anticipate receiving anywhere from $2,000 to $250,000-plus, depending on the program.

Other perks of being awarded a grant include additional exposure, possible mentoring, training, workshops, other services, and more. According to grantsforwomen.org, "Women are underserved and overlooked, and suffer continuously from unfair practices. Women grants, especially business grants for women, give them the upper hand to fight back, and prevail. This type of assistance enables them to recover from an unfair and unjust system that has existed for a long time. The concept is very similar to affirmative action initiatives that help other minority groups."

Additional sources of funding we've discussed previously include crowdfunding, entering pitch competitions, and working with traditional lenders. There are a couple of crowdfunding sites that are even geared specifically toward women, including WomenYouShouldFund and IFundWomen.

In general, when it comes to funding, women need to shift their mindset to become more aggressive touting their ideas and their brands and actively seeking additional investors without worrying about what others will think of them. Aim high and put yourself out there—that's what men (and successful business owners) do!

Know Your Numbers

According to a recent Capital One study, women need to know their own numbers inside and out before approaching potential investors.[18] Of course, it is critical to understand your company's finances thoroughly before setting out to secure funding, and thankfully, the vast majority of female business owners are in that position. As reported by the Small Business Growth Index, 94 percent of women feel confident when it comes to understanding their companies' finances.[19]

Leverage Connections and Pitch

Female entrepreneurs should build their network by forming connections with people in banking, friends, associates, and others in their community. Be sure to talk with them about your startup and goals. Go back to your elevator pitch and really be able to explain your business clearly and succinctly in 30 seconds. Include what makes it unique, and be tenacious. Don't give up when you hear a *no*! You'll eventually get a *yes* if you have your facts in order and stick with your plan.

When you're pitching, research the investment group that you're interested in before you approach them. Find out what their values and reputation are as well as what type of companies they invest in. Think about everything we discussed in Mindset Shift 1 and the little things, too, like body language and getting into the right mindset before you begin talking. Practice beforehand so that you have it down. You can record your pitch on your phone or via a video conference platform to see how you did. I often do this when I am getting ready for something big.

Assess your business's weaknesses and get ready for inquiries related to them, as it's important to come armed and informed. Prepare to be outnumbered by a panel, and brainstorm potential questions that may be asked and how you'll respond. Additionally, be sure to ask for feedback if you get a rejection.

It's important to set up meetings with multiple potential investors so that you have several chances to make your pitch. This will put the odds more in your favor. You can even create a system related to it by ranking the investment groups that you would like to get involved with in order from your top choice to your bottom choice. Schedule an appointment with the bottom choice on your list first so that you can get practice before you approach the one that you want to make a deal with the most. No matter what, make the best use of the meeting time you've been granted at every group. Reflect upon the selling tips I mentioned previously (such as overcoming your fears, being well prepared, and making personal connections). A big part of your job here is building rapport with your audience, so endeavor to really connect with them and show them why they should do business with you as well as how your startup stands out from others. Once again, you have to outshine your competitors!

Don't think of obtaining funding as something that you will only need to participate in at the start of your venture either. This constant focus on capital attainment is vital to your growth as an entrepreneur. There will be other times when you are further along that you may need additional funds and investors to take your startup to the next level. Perhaps you will want to expand your geographical location or grow your product or service line; you may require extra capital to do so. Keep this part of the Mindset Shift—being open to and comfortable with seeking funds and potential investors—an ongoing part of running your business as you continue to shift your money mindset, you financial maven, you!

FINAL THOUGHTS

You are a fiscally competent fempreneur who is ready to make the attitude shift necessary to cultivate financial confidence. You're putting yourself out there and growing. As we've discussed, it begins with looking at the psychological influences that are associated with your money mindset by first recognizing old ways of thinking and bad habits and addressing and eliminating fears related to finances, such as living from paycheck to paycheck or groundless uncertainty about your financial future.

Stop viewing money as a taboo topic and learn to get comfortable talking about it, embracing the fact that money is a means to achieve the lifestyle that you desire and to be able to take care of the people that are most important to you. What's more, you deserve financial success—you really do! Part of this phase of the Mindset Shift will also involve critically analyzing your current economic situation and then developing fiscal targets and goals. You'll have to budget and cut costs both at your business and in your personal life to make this happen.

Lastly, you'll utilize and amplify methods such as bootstrapping, negotiation, and raising capital to take a tighter grip on the financial reins of your startup and move toward greater levels of profitability. You've got this!

ORGANIZING YOUR TIME

s a new fempreneur, you are going to be busy! You will struggle to find time to get everything done, particularly if you are a solopreneur and doing most of the work by yourself. You will also be juggling many responsibilities, often performing multiple roles at your startup. This persistent pull will be compounded by the fact that there are also fewer boundaries with our always-on world, so you'll feel like you have to be constantly connected. Dealing with continuous transformation and addressing numerous undertakings simultaneously will be your new norm as an active business owner. Does this realization make your head spin? You're not alone, but I assure you: you *can* master this mild chaos by taking control. We will work on that together with our fourth Mindset Shift.

The Mindset Shift we'll discuss in this chapter focuses on how female founders need to think about time management and organization. The reality is that although all new business owners are busy, women entrepreneurs face additional challenges in this arena, juggling countless responsibilities as heads of their family and heads of their business. According to the Pew Research Center, "women still bear a heavier load than men in balancing work and family."[1] Another study found that "a lack of the effective division of domestic labor was the single largest contributor of entrepreneurial failure for women, playing a role in 49% of the failures . . . studied."[2] As such, this Mindset Shift is crucial for your ultimate success as an entrepreneur. We'll get into a few strategies to help you master your time, including goal setting, scheduling, aiming for work-life balance, and dropping guilt. Sound good? I hope you're reading this book while soaking in a nice lavender bubble bath!

Setting Goals

The best way to begin this balancing act is by setting goals. Establishing realistic business targets is vital for female entrepreneurs—and requires a Mindset Shift to achieve. You'll need to break your goals down into daily, monthly, and yearly milestones and benchmarks, and ensure that they are SMART. SMART goals are important because they are unambiguous, set within your reach, and attached to a schedule in order to accomplish them by a fixed date. SMART goals are also helpful because they give you a precise target to aim for and enable you to clarify certain questions such as what, when, where, and why you want to achieve this goal. They also allow you to measure your progress and determine whether or not you have achieved the target you've set for yourself. By making the goal realistic, you won't be reaching for milestones that are impossible to hit.

An example of a general goal is "I want to get more sales," but an example of a SMART goal is "I want to increase sales of our new products by 5 percent within the next six months through increasing daily sales calls by 30 percent and implementing a new social media advertising campaign on Twitter and Instagram."

SMART goals are effective for founders because they enable you to establish exact benchmarks for different areas of your startup. This will allow you to streamline tasks and make sure that you are not losing sight of any facets of your business. If you have team members, these goals will also enable you to delegate appropriately and can generally act as a compass to measure whether you are on course with getting your business to where you want it to be. The more detailed the goals are, the better your blueprint for success. Another perk of goal setting is that these types of specific targets thwart procrastination by holding you accountable for what you set out to do.

Although adhering to your goals is crucial for success, it's also important to point out that you need to build in some flexibility, as things will come up that you cannot predict. It may be necessary for you to alter your plans and adjust from time to time—and that is OK. The COVID-19 pandemic is the perfect example of this. Most entrepreneurs had targets in mind, but when the virus shook our entire world, those targets needed to shift. I've been thrown a curve ball or two, and you will as well. Be willing to adjust as needed.

Some early objectives that you'll set as a new fempreneur may be related to your business plan, the creation of your website and social media accounts, revenue attainment, product launch, forming connections with suppliers, and establishing a networking or sales strategy, to name a few. Benjamin Franklin said famously, "By failing to prepare, you are preparing to fail." Make sure that planning and setting SMART goals are always at the heart of your processes and forward momentum as a business owner because they are a central part to this Mindset Shift.

Create Action Plans

In business, you must also develop action plans, which are documents that list the steps needed to achieve a target or benchmark that aligns with your short- and long-term goals. When developing an action plan, you must take into account priorities, deadlines, responsible parties, and necessary resources and then incorporate the ability to track progress within your plan. Typically, an action plan will be in a template format and include columns outlining the following:

- Your objectives: what you want to put into action
- Related tasks: what you need to do to attain your goals
- Success criteria: how you'll measure attainment or progress
- Necessary resources: what you need to accomplish your goals
- Microsteps: actions you will take to execute your objectives as well as related tasks
- Time frame for completion: how long it will take to make it happen or when you hope to accomplish it

You might even create your own modified template (including the information listed here) or search for one online so that you have a basic, consistent outline for all of your action plans. Why not give your master list a catchy name like Mary's Must-Dos or Donna's Dealmakers? It'll spice 'em up a bit.

Action plans are important because they give you well-defined direction on how and when you are going to hit your targets, including what's needed, who will perform each task, and when the task must be complete. You can also utilize project management software to help you stay on top of and organize your projects. Some popular choices include Basecamp, EverNote, and Trello. I've used Trello for many projects, and I find it quite helpful and user-friendly, and when utilizing this software, you can move a task from one team member to another. Getting something off your plate and onto someone else's is not only satisfying, but it also gives you a little mental boost, sort of like crossing an item off a list or cleaning out the fridge. Goodbye, leftover pizza!

Fancy tools, although nice, are not necessary, as you can use an Excel spreadsheet or Word document for these purposes as well. So don't spend unnecessarily if you have limited funds (remember what we talked about in the last Mindset Shift about spending your money wisely).

Once you get your action plans structured, break the plans down into the microsteps that it will take to make them happen. For each action plan, there will be a number of stages required to hit the goal. The more detailed your microsteps, the better chance you'll have of accomplishing the benchmarks that you've set for yourself and your business. For example, writing a blog post might be one of your action plans, but there will be multiple steps to accomplish it, including brainstorming about the topic, creating an outline, doing research, writing the post, editing the post, choosing a picture to accompany it, posting it, and finally sharing it.

When you break your action plans down into microsteps, they seem much more manageable and digestible, and there is a clear place to start and finish. It's the ultimate productivity road map and how-to guide. Creating and utilizing action plans and microsteps is a priority for this entrepreneurial Mindset Shift.

Schedule and Review Your Plans

After you've created your action plans and microsteps, it will all boil down to scheduling and review. In terms of scheduling, it's important to set deadlines and hold yourself accountable. Sometimes just the act of putting it down in writing is all the forward momentum that you need.

When it's time to review your progress, be honest in your self-assessments. Don't give yourself an A+ when you deserve a C (we see you). Really make note of what you are on track with and areas that you need to improve. Use your calendar and other visual cues and reminders to help you stay on task. One of the best ways to do this is to add tasks to your calendar as soon as you implement your action plan and microsteps. This will ensure you won't delay your progress and will be consistent.

You'll want to begin chipping away at your action plans and become more productive, so it will be helpful to work in chunks and minimize distractions. As part of your daily routine, identify three to five must-dos every day. Make this list at the beginning of the week for the whole week and then again at the start of each day. Schedule chunks (in one- to two-hour blocks) to accomplish the three to five items that you've pinpointed, and then check back in with yourself at the end of the day to hold yourself accountable for your progress. Block out those chunks on your calendar so that you have time dedicated specifically for accomplishing these must-dos. If you don't finish everything slotted, you'll have to move the incomplete tasks to the next day. If you are ahead of schedule and have extra time, shift toward completing other items on your weekly list. The most significant thing here is to make sure that you are checking in with yourself in terms of your progress and adjusting to be as productive as possible.

Plan for Everything

As an organized startup leader, you should have master checklists associated with everything that you want to accomplish. Checklist tracking is a critical part of your process; review your checklists in the morning and then again in the evening, as well as weekly for an overview of bigger-picture items. Get creative with them so they're visually appealing and you actually *want* to interact with them. I mean, why not throw some glitter their way (the virtual kind of course—the other stuff's too messy!).

Document and categorize all of your to-dos into these checklists as they come in and revisit them often, evaluating each in terms of the time, energy, and resources needed as well as their priority. Cross items off the list one by one as time allows and have a weekly review with yourself where you clarify outcomes, keep track of your progress, and determine what's next. Organize and plan, and you will accomplish the goals and benchmarks that you've set for yourself, adjusting as necessary if you are falling short.

You are in the driver's seat when it comes to your ultimate success. So hit the gas pedal—stopping periodically to check the engine and fuel up—to drive your results!

Maintain Perspective

Learn to look at both the grand scheme and the day-to-day. Reward yourself for accomplishing goals and small tasks along the way, which will reinforce that productive behavior. Did you complete all of the items on an action plan or finish all of the tasks on your daily to-do list? Yes? Then treat yourself to a facial, or go for a walk, or order a movie. Hell, buy yourself a lemon cupcake and down it with a glass of pinot! You deserve it, girl! You might even just tell yourself that you did a great job. No matter how small your reward, celebrating your productivity and accomplishment is key. Remember, focus is critical and productivity is what will make things happen for you as a woman business owner. Fempreneurs work smarter and get what they want out of life, and you are a rising fempreneur!

Plan Ahead

As you schedule your microsteps and goals, be sure to work ahead and plan for busy periods. When you know you have a heavy week coming up, perhaps one with a lot of travel and events, get in front of it by having presentations and other reports prepared well ahead of time. That way, you will have extra hours available if any emergencies or time-sensitive tasks get thrown on top of your already busy week.

Can you think of a time when that happened to you in the past, when you left everything to the last minute only to have a few catastrophes arise when you were trying to get your work done (like your printer not working or your child getting sick)? We've all been there, but no more! You're a time-savvy entrepreneur now—one who likes to plan as much as possible so these situations are unlikely to happen to you again. This extreme preparation and planning are central to this entrepreneurial Mindset Shift.

Tackle the "Meh" First

When beginning on any large task or project, deal with the mundane first. You know, those things that we put off because we don't like doing them. Doing them *first* will eliminate some roadblocks (mental and otherwise) and give us the forward momentum to get the project off the ground. As they say at Nike, just do it!

Try to move things off of your mental checklist and desk as quickly as possible to prevent them from slowing you down. For example, if you have a stack of bills sitting waiting for you, pay them quickly, file or shred them, and go on to your next thing. Look at that nice clean spot on your desk now! If you have a bunch of small emails that you can respond to swiftly and easily, do so and get them out of your inbox. Just having them sitting in there is stressing you out whether you realize it or not. Reply—delete. Forward—delete. Ahhhh . . . isn't that satisfying?

Put Yourself in Check

As a business owner, you'll always be watching your numbers: sales, revenue, collections, and so on. Are you on track in terms of progress? If not, what do you need to adjust in order to get there? Put these progress check-ins on your calendar as well. It's so easy to do now and can be set up in your email program or on your smartphone. How often and what dates or times will you check in? Weekly, monthly, or otherwise? Attach a funny sound to these alerts so that they make you laugh while prompting you to take action—maybe a silly phrase like Dunkin's "It's time to make the donuts" or lyrics from the song "She works hard for the money" by Donna Summer—whatever gives you a smile and motivates you to achieve.

Improving Your Time Management

Female entrepreneurs often understandably have a difficult time with scheduling due to a heavier load. As revealed by the Pew Research Center, they must balance issues related to managing their family while juggling all of the household obligations they are responsible for as well as those tasks and commitments related to running their startups.[3] This section will show you how to outline and schedule your daily tasks and commitments. We'll also discuss improving focus, setting weekly review time to clarify business objectives, tracking progress, and reducing time-sucks.

Time management is certainly challenging, but you can make adjustments. Some of the many things that you can do to maximize your time as an entrepreneur include minimizing disruptions, slowing down to take a breath, incorporating small breaks throughout the day, and avoiding the urge to do everything flawlessly; done is much, much better than flawless, so aim for 95 percent amazing vs. 100 percent impeccable. Focus on your personal productivity first and foremost, and pay attention to your daily work habits. What throws you off track? Notifications on your phone? Place it across the room. Emails coming in? Sign out. Googling things that come to mind randomly? Learn to thwart this type of behavior. You can even come up with a mantra that you repeat to yourself when you catch yourself getting off track, like my favorite, telling myself, "Charlene, get back to work!" The more you focus, the more productive you'll be, and you'll actually be able to get more done in less time. And, ding, ding, guess what? That means more time for you and other important people in your life. Did someone say girls' night?

Take Five

Taking breaks is critical, as counterintuitive as it may seem. The reality is that when you leave your workspace for a moment, you are resetting your mind and focus, and will come back to your desk with a more refreshed and attentive outlook. So, get up from time to time, stretch your legs, grab a glass of water, or step outside to get some air for a minute. Sit on the patio and soak in the day. Play your favorite song on YouTube and do a little dance in your office—you've still got the moves. It will help you maintain your focus, and as I've mentioned, focus is the name of the game when it comes to being productive.

Tidy Up

Work hard to declutter your workspace. By streamlining, you will be able to physically get items off your desk and/or tackle your mental checklist more quickly. This applies to both your work area as well as the files and organization on your laptop. Have you ever wasted an hour trying to find a document you misplaced under a stack of papers? Or had trouble locating a file you knew you'd already started? The tidier your work environment, the less time you'll waste moving from task to task and trying to locate things. So, clean up your entrepreneurial act (so to speak)!

Ditch Distractions

Again, you will need to train yourself to really focus and eliminate interruptions. Do this by silencing notifications on your devices and resisting the urge to surf the web or talk on the phone. Strive to complete things quickly and with your full concentration, and using this method, you'll get more done in less time.

If you know you should be able to accomplish more than you are right now, look at your entire schedule critically. Identify areas that are sucking time away from you; Netflix-binging perhaps? (That new series can wait!) Spending hours on social media? (Schedule time after hours to catch up on Insta and TikTok instead of during work time. Maybe limit it to Tuesdays and Saturdays from 6 to 8 p.m.) The best way to find out where your time is being spent is to track yourself for an entire week. You may be surprised at how much time you're wasting without getting anything in return.

Find More Time

Wouldn't it be nice to have more time in a day? It's possible if you really look at your schedule and see where you can cut some things. Meetings are a prime example of this. Only meet when necessary. You can often accomplish what you want with a quick email exchange or phone call instead of a long meeting.

What else is squandering your time? Do you have an exorbitant amount of administrative paperwork? Can you outsource it? Are there certain tasks that take away from other activities that are more important to your bottom line? Then recruit some help or get creative with how you can reduce them. Do you lose focus and spend more time getting things done because you're not working efficiently? Track and modify your work habits to eliminate wasted minutes.

Maintaining Your Self-Care and Work-Life Balance

When it comes to our fourth Mindset Shift, self-care is the third leg of the tripod, along with goal setting and time management. Proper work-life balance benefits female entrepreneurs in all aspects of their lives. This section will offer a number of steps that you can take as a woman business owner to improve your work-life balance, including setting limits to avoid overcommitting; making time for the people and activities that are important to you; prioritizing basic health needs; communicating about your boundaries and plans with key stakeholders to obtain buy-in; and getting a handle on your schedule, projects, and work environment.

As a busy fempreneur, you must take care of yourself—your health, well-being, and needs. The happier and stronger you are as an individual, the more you will thrive in business and increase your positive interactions with others. This involves your critical need for work-life balance. Proper work-life balance is advantageous for founders in many ways and is so crucial for overall happiness. There are many steps that a woman can take to improve her work-life balance, but here are some of my favorite tips.

Love Yourself

Loving yourself is at the heart of balance. This love involves self-care, putting your needs at the top of your priority list, and being kind and patient with *you*. Balance helps women in their personal lives by giving them time for what's special to them without feeling overextended or guilty. It helps them as fempreneurs, as they will need to avoid excessive fatigue and have the strength to keep forging ahead. Love yourself enough to make balance a priority in your life.

Put Proper Limits in Place

The best way to deal with too many demands is to set appropriate boundaries and make time for the people and things that are most important to you. Let everyone know where they stand and what your limits are. Establish a daily start and stop time for work and develop a standing schedule. Communication with interested parties, whether they are friends, family, clients, or others, is the key here. Get them on board with your boundaries and plans, and tell them how you intend to find time for them, where they fit in, and how important their buy-in is to you. You'll be surprised at how supportive they'll be.

Stay Healthy

It's critical that we take care of ourselves. Neglecting our sleep and over-all health can be a symptom of imbalance in our lives. A higher level of self-care will help us to make better use of our time; feel more content; juggle multiple priorities; and be more productive, optimistic, and focused. Incorporate fitness, breaks, and activities to stimulate your mind, body, and soul.

In the words of relationship consultant Barbara DeAngelis, "Women need real moments of solitude and self-reflection to balance out how much of ourselves we give away."[4] Amen. I know that I feel as if I am constantly giving pieces of myself away. I'm sure you feel the same. Let's fix that. Do you enjoy meditation, yoga, reading, taking courses, or Pilates? Even something as simple as a short nap can do wonders for your outlook and well-being. Schedule time for healthy meals and relaxation techniques as well. Get back to the basics, like drinking enough water and eating your fruits and vegetables. Remember what your momma taught you!

Don't Overcommit

We also need to be aware of committing to more than we should and failing to delegate, outsource, or otherwise get additional help. If you don't like to do a certain task, hire or ask someone else to do it if possible. Look for ways to share other responsibilities as well; there are likely many people who'd love to pitch in, in both your personal and professional life. When in doubt or when you feel overwhelmed, outsource!

Pay someone to do your laundry (doesn't that sound magical?) or watch your children for a few hours (i.e., let you work in peace) while you focus on activities that will bring in more revenue. Pair up with a friend and take turns with childcare. Order your groceries and other items online so that you spend less time running errands. Better yet, if you are going to head out, schedule your errands in blocks (i.e., run four or five during a couple of hours instead of one at a time) so that your days aren't interrupted.

Learn to Say No!

As part of not overcommitting, you will need to get comfortable with saying no. You can't possibly do everything, and that's okay. Don't feel guilty about turning down things that you simply don't have time for and/or don't really want to do anyhow. Not feeling the bake sale? Ditch it. If you don't want to take on an additional project (that doesn't offer you much in return), then decline it politely.

You will have to pick and choose where you are spending your time, so only make room on your schedule for those things that are high on your priority list. Adjust your mindset so you don't feel bad for saying no to things that you don't want to do, that don't serve you or your business, or that you don't really have time for. You can't do everything, so be smart with your choices.

Take Control

Greater work-life balance can be achieved by taking the reins on your journey: scheduling wisely by working on projects in pieces, eliminating and reducing disturbances, and incorporating self-management techniques. Some best practices include scheduling all aspects of your day, identifying (and eliminating) timewasters, and remembering to save some time for *you*. Take a day off here and there, and remember to spend time with those who are most important to you while still attending to and growing your business. When these two areas are in balance, you will thrive and so will your startup.

Drop Guilt

This is a biggie. Let's face it, as women and particularly as fempreneurs, we are always feeling guilty about something. In fact, we feel guilty for just about everything—having too much fun, not having enough fun, being too good at something, not being good enough, the way we look, the success we have (or don't), and so much more. Further, numerous studies have proven that women are more prone to guilt than men.[5]

There is both social guilt—guilt placed upon us by society and the people in our lives—and individual guilt, which is self-imposed when we don't live up to our own expectations. Are we not spending enough time on our business (or too much?), did we forget to send an email that we meant to, neglect to buy a get-well gift for Uncle Jim, or not help a friend last week when we really wanted to? Do you worry continuously about spending enough quality time with your children or spouse? Stop beating yourself up! You are not superwoman, and there is no way to do everything that you want to. And no one does! No one!

You Can Balance

Former first lady Michelle Obama summed up the importance of work-life balance well by saying, "Women, in particular, need to keep an eye on their physical and mental health, because if we're scurrying to and from appointments and errands, we don't have a lot of time to take care of ourselves. We need to do a better job of putting ourselves higher on our own 'to do' list."[6]

As a fempreneur, striving for work-life balance is vital to mastering this time management Mindset Shift. Being a business owner is challenging and lonely. You will have a lot of ups and downs on your journey and not much help growing your startup. But the balance you create for yourself will give you the strength you need to keep charging ahead. The temptation to overwork will always be there for you, but working too long will actually cause you to be less productive. Instead, make sure that you find the time for other areas of your life that are important to you so that you can enjoy them while growing your company.

And balance can be achieved—I'm living proof! I'm a single mother with two girls. I have a full-time job, work a side gig, and write books in my free time. (What free time?) I know a thing or two about being stretched, pulled, and feeling guilty. I've been at this for years. I'll be in the middle of something I'm working on for a client when someone throws something extra on my plate at work, my daughter screams for me to break up a fight she's having in another room with my other daughter, all while I'm thinking about my dad's birthday (I need to call him, send a card) and remembering that I also need to reach out to my friend whose father passed away last week. Shoot, and I haven't worked out yet today either. It's okay.

Think about all of the steps we talked about in this chapter and take control of that schedule. Look at each item in terms of its priority and where it fits into those daily plans. You can make it all work. Get creative with it and never allow yourself to feel bullied by other people's expectations of you, or worse yet, those placed on you by yourself. You are an amazing business owner, mother, friend, spouse, and strategist!

The most essential thing to remember about work-life balance is that no one is going to do it for you, so *you* have to make it a priority and talk to the other important people in your life about your schedule. The more in balance you are, the more successful your business will be!

FINAL THOUGHTS

As we've discussed, this Mindset Shift is all about organizing your time as a fempreneur. It begins with goal setting and then breaking those benchmarks down into action plans and the microsteps that it will take to accomplish them; think both short- and long-term here. Be sure to check in on your metrics and progress along the way, always attacking your day by optimizing your schedule and productivity. Lastly, put an extreme focus on work-life balance and self-care and ditch unfounded and unnecessary guilt as it relates to your schedule and obligations. Bear in mind the words of Margaret Thatcher, the former prime minister of Britain, "If you want something said, ask a man: if you want something done, ask a woman."[7] Be that strong woman, use what you've learned, and keep getting things done!

BRANDING AND BUILDING PRESENCE

Y ou are an amazing, smart, kind, savvy fempreneur! Do you shout it from the rooftops? No? You're not alone. Another area in which female entrepreneurs often need a Mindset Shift relates to branding and building presence. It's particularly vital when you first launch a startup, as building presence is the very thing that gets your company off the ground. In fact, it's the entry ticket for just about every new business endeavor today. Unfortunately, a recent study revealed that women are much less inclined to self-promote than men.[1] Another study found that "women find it harder to trumpet their accomplishments."[2]

This chapter will guide you in how to achieve the fifth Mindset Shift through topics such as personal branding, networking, and building visibility—in other words, *growing* you and then *showing* you!

Personal Branding

According to a *Harvard Business Review* article, "personal branding has some unique challenges for female professionals. Research has repeatedly shown that women are subject to a phenomenon known as the 'likability conundrum.' Gender norms presume that women should be agreeable, warm, and nurturing, and when they violate these norms—such as when they step up to make a tough decision, share a strong opinion, or promote themselves—they're often penalized for that behavior in a way that men wouldn't be."[3] Since personal branding involves self-promotion, this can be an additional challenge point for new female entrepreneurs.

It can be tricky for women to talk about their accomplishments, particularly in the workplace where we are judged in a harsher light than men for doing so. Many women eventually realize, at some point, however, that they won't get the opportunities that they deserve without telling others about their strong performance and accomplishments. I've lived it and made that transition myself. This section will help you to make the Mindset Shift to begin to develop your personal brand—which showcases your expertise, experience, personality, philosophies, thought leadership, and more—through brainstorming and research into the most effective way to present yourself digitally.

Personal branding can be intimidating at first, but like so many of the things that we've discussed before, it comes down to planning and execution. Perhaps the best place to start is to brainstorm about and begin to develop your personal branding angle. Everyone needs a personal brand today (particularly entrepreneurs), but the concept of a personal brand was first introduced by Tom Peters. Now widely quoted, Peters said, "Regardless of age, regardless of position, regardless of the business we happen to be in, all of us need to understand the importance of branding. We are CEOs of our own companies: Me Inc. To be in business today, our most important job is to be head marketer for the brand called You."[4]

Personal branding encompasses all of the marketing and promotion of yourself, including the qualities and traits that you bring to the table. Your personal brand highlights your expertise, experience, personality, charm, philosophies, and more. It's your job to take control of how you want to be seen and how you want to present yourself, both critical aspects of this fifth Mindset Shift.

As business and marketing expert Seth Godin famously said, "People do not buy goods and services, they buy relations, stories, and magic."[5] Tell the magical story of you—your own unique blend of charisma, skills, experience, and that little something extra (*lagniappe*, as they say in New Orleans) that no one else has. If you need a bit of personal-branding inspiration, look to some of the personal-branding masters like Oprah Winfrey, Lady Gaga, or Martha Stewart. What comes to mind when you think of each of these women, and what steps did they take to make it so?

One way to start is to Google yourself. What did you find? The same search results will come back for customers and potential clients searching for you, so you want to maximize what others see and say about you.

As a first step in fine-tuning your personal brand, you should develop your value proposition statement. Approach writing it as you would with any other "product." I bet you never thought of yourself as a product, but you are! Your value proposition will focus on your USP (unique selling proposition).

When it comes to working on the USP for your personal brand, concentrate on three key areas that you want to be known for. Are you a strategy or marketing expert? Does your knowledge lie in health care, business technology, or yoga? For me, my USP would involve being an author and speaker, as well as a business, branding, and entrepreneurship mentor. Give some thought to the topics that most closely align with your skills and strengths, as well as your business, as they will be a major part of your USP. You will use this information to create a two- to three-sentence statement that describes what you have that sets you apart (again, your experience, abilities, knowledge, qualities). Your value proposition identifies who you are, what you do, and the value you bring to those you interact with—so put some polish on it (the extra shiny kind).

Next, come up with three to four keywords that you would use to describe yourself. This task might be a little more challenging because we often struggle to pinpoint exactly how to define ourselves; we can usually see others more clearly. Is it your ability to connect with people, your willingness to go the extra mile, or your unwavering reliability? Several of my keywords include *personable*, *supportive*, *innovative*, and *tenacious*. Again, these traits will be unique for everyone; the key here is to focus on and draw attention to what it is about you that will be most appealing to your potential clients. You'll be using these keywords to help describe yourself and your brand repeatedly.

After that, you'll pinpoint your values and passion. Your passion is a subject or topic that you feel strongly about or are an authority in, and your values are the principles that you hold yourself to or things that you hold in high regard. As an example, I am passionate about entrepreneurship as a lucrative path for women, living life to the fullest, my daughters, and empowering others to live their best lives! I value honesty, innovation, hard work, fairness, and kindness. How about you?

Finally, craft your elevator pitch. I know that we hear the term "elevator pitch" so often today it might seem to be a cliché, but that doesn't negate its value. Every entrepreneur needs a good elevator pitch, as you never know when an opportunity will come up. You must be able to present yourself and your business succinctly and clearly at any time. So create your three- to four-sentence pitch to use when you meet someone new—on an airplane, at an event, or, surprise, surprise, in an elevator. It should be a concise summary of your skills, background, and what you hope to accomplish. Look to your value proposition, passion, values, and keywords for clues.

When developing your personal brand, don't be afraid to phone a friend. They'll easily be able to give keywords and other information that define you, and they might see your strengths differently than you do, providing some solid advice or anecdotes. Also reach out to your existing clients, as they can tell you what the best part of working with you is. Combine all of this information together to further fine-tune your value proposition statement and pitch.

For example, my pitch goes something like this: "I am a supportive business and branding mentor, author, consultant, and trainer. I help individuals and businesses achieve their goals and objectives through collaboration and tactical planning. I am passionate about innovation, entrepreneurship for women, and living life to the fullest." As it relates to your personal brand, always lead with your strengths and you will shine.

When your brainstorming is complete, you'll formulate your personal branding goals by listing at least two targets that you have for yourself in terms of building your personal brand. This can be anything from getting your social media profiles set up to getting a head shot to growing your following to becoming more active on certain platforms. (These personal-branding goals should be a part of the SMART goals we talked about in the last Mindset Shift.) You can also think about it in terms of committing to creating more thought leadership pieces or joining new networking groups. The objective here is to really make your personal brand stand out and to shine the spotlight on yourself as an expert, leader, and innovator.

Personal branding encompasses so much, including projecting charisma so that people will want to be around you, network with you, and ultimately do business with you. This charisma includes calling people by name; using good manners; and being polite, likeable, professional, charming, and well groomed. It's also important that you keep up on current events and industry trends and infuse humor into your conversations and online presence. Who doesn't love a good joke or a smile to brighten up an average day? So show them the funny, honey! The person who gets the smile, gets the in. It's up to you to grab hold of your brand because it's not something that anyone else will do for you. Your brand is your responsibility and is instrumental to your shifting fempreneur mindset.

So, think about all of the ways that you can showcase your capabilities and skills. How are you ensuring that others know about you and that you'll be top of mind when they have a need for someone like you? Here are a few tips:

1. **Get creative.** How can you get your message out in a way that is unique and attracts attention?
2. **Insert yourself.** Strategize about where and how you can get into the mix.
3. **Specialize.** Narrow down the areas that you are most knowledgeable in. Then focus on portraying yourself as an expert in relation to each by generating related content on a regular basis. The process of doing so will provide value to those in your network and grow your following.
4. **Be visible.** They'll never hear about you if you're hiding in an office. Put yourself out there in person, by video, and online.
5. **Enlighten others.** You must provide useful ideas and opinions to pull people in. Share resources and spread positivity.
6. **Be consistent.** Develop a routine to boost your personal brand. Communicate and post on your social platforms weekly. Be sure to push content out on a continual basis as well. Your following and presence won't grow overnight but will increase over time with thoughtful planning.
7. **Give to receive.** The more that you give your talent and energy to others, the more you'll build your brand and get support back in return. Be generous with your skills.

Networking

Who do you know? That's the million-dollar question. Women with an entrepreneurial mindset understand the importance of networking as a business owner and leader—through forums such as webinars, digital discussions, conferences, business groups, industry associations, and other events. In this section we'll get into some methods to help you improve your networking-specific communication skills, build trust with potential clients and other stakeholders, connect with influencers, and form personal branding strategic alliances to grow your circle of connection while building recognition as a thought leader—all paramount to completing this Mindset Shift.

For startup founders, networking is critical. Much of it you'll do online and much of it, during nonpandemic times, you'll do in person. Get out there and attend conferences, join associations, and listen to what others in your industry have to say. I guarantee you that at every workshop or online webinar you attend, you'll walk away with at least a few tips. I always do; I love hearing what others have to say. Find out what entrepreneurs in your network are doing and try to replicate their successes. People are willing to share; you need only listen. You might also want to get to know other members and business owners and join a smaller networking/support group. I am in a group of five professional women who meet once a month to share best practices and successes as we move our entrepreneurial ventures forward. We all met at an association conference and really hit it off. We have been meeting for several years and have all benefited from the support.

When it comes to networking, you have to focus on your communication. Ask yourself important questions, such as how are you regularly interacting with people in your network? How have you provided someone with value this week? Can you obtain a leadership position with a professional or philanthropic organization? Are you taking advantage of growing your contacts on social media platforms? Zig Ziglar, the iconic sales guru, said, "If people like you, they will listen to you, but if they trust you, they'll do business with you."[6] Do what you can to earn and build that trust.

You might also want to consider creating a personal ethics statement as part of that trust building. In it, you can include information about your core values, beliefs, and opinions as well as what it's like to work with you. It should be about one to two paragraphs long and showcase what value you'll bring to customers as well as how you'll treat them fairly. It may be just the thing that makes clients decide to partner with you instead of your competitors.

Don't be afraid to connect either. You'd likely be amazed at some of the connections that I've made on LinkedIn, Instagram, and Twitter by simply reaching out and interacting with people. I'm often invited on their podcasts or shows and to do guest blogs, and many have reached out to me because we've had things in common, as it works both ways. When you get invested in a certain association, you'll meet plenty of their members, and they'll look forward to seeing you at other events. You'll also find that the same groups tend to frequent particular conferences. Take advantage and work together. You can form personal-branding strategic alliances and feature or mention them in your posts, and they'll feature and mention you as well. Remember, when you give, you often get something back in return, so give a lot.

Be sure to get to know and embrace influencers, too, as they are easier to find and link up with today than ever before. They will be affiliated with big brands, and in some cases, they are the big brand. Influencers are easy to spot online through their large followings and high level of engagement, so gain a few as allies.

Networking is a deposit in the bank of your future and in your startup. It won't happen immediately, but if you do it right, you will continue to receive its dividends for years. I, for one, can network with the best of them! You can too.

Building Visibility

Women entrepreneurs also need to prioritize building their visibility and industry presence—not only when they're launching their new business, but as their venture grows. This section will walk you through this critical facet of the fifth Mindset Shift, which involves developing a thought leadership presence so that you are viewed as an expert on a certain subject or within a specific industry. Thought leadership is a key way to boost visibility in a sector while establishing and increasing your general profile as a leader.

Become a Thought Leader

When it comes to building your presence, one of the best things that you can do is to develop your skills in the area of thought leadership. A thought leader is a person who is known as an authority within a particular space. Creating thought leadership content does exactly what the name implies: it establishes you as an expert. Your thought leadership content should discuss your ideas and opinions on important topics, industry trends, technology, and areas of expertise, and it can be presented in a number of ways.

One of the easiest paths to begin is by creating a blog. Blogs can be part of an existing website, and many hosting services have blog capabilities built right in. Come up with a creative name for your blog and then break the content down into three to four subject areas. My blog is called "Entrepreneurship, Life Enthusiasm, and Energizing Your Brand." It focuses on the topics of business and branding, personal growth and inspiration, and entrepreneurship. I also have some posts related to being a single parent and a survivor called "Single Parent Snippets," which correspond with my other book, a personal memoir on love and overcoming tragedy. Writing blog posts is a good way to start because you have the most control and are able to schedule your content out over a period of time. It's also a less intimidating way to begin compared to other options. You should blog at least once a week if not more and be consistent so that your subscribers know when they can expect new content. You're so smart and charming that they'll really begin to look forward to it too.

Contribute to Media Outlets

Another way that you can establish yourself as a thought leader is to contribute to media outlets. These outlets often seek experts to comment on articles that they are writing or want to include additional quotes in. There are also a number of organizations and agencies that help match writers and experts, such as HARO (Help a Reporter Out). I have contributed to a lot of articles through HARO and have made a number of contacts that way as well. I highly recommend it as a good method to build your presence. There are other similar organizations, such as ProfNet, Source Bottle, Pitch Rate, and Media Kitty, that you can look into, too. You can also pitch entire articles directly to media outlets, but be sure to follow and adhere to their submission guidelines as standards vary and they tend to be particular about them. I have taken this path as well, and there is certainly a lot of value in it.

Become an Author

When it comes to being seen as a thought leader or expert, one of the surest ways is to write a book. People are becoming authors at an increasing rate due to the rise in the number of publishing options available. You can decide whether to go with a traditional publisher, a self-publishing service, or a hybrid publisher (which is a combination of the two). Depending on your goals and objectives, some options will be more appealing to you than others. Many experts even consider a book akin to a business card these days. It's a vehicle that can be used to increase your brand and presence and really does the most to establish you as an expert. I've written two books, and I can attest to their power.

Self-publishing is faster than traditional publishing, but the author is responsible for everything. Hiring a company to assist you can ease the burden, but authors who go that direction should research their chosen company very carefully, as it's a bit of a no-man's-land when it comes to people offering to help you publish your book.

If you decide to go the traditional publishing route, you'll need to first write a book proposal. It's sort of daunting—like writing a dissertation—but well worth it. It will include information such as an overview of your book, target audience (who'll read it), market analysis, competitive analysis (showing which books like it already exist on the market and where your book fits in), the table of contents, chapter summaries, and sample chapters (usually one or two). The traditional publishing path is a longer process than self-publishing, so you will need to display grit and persistence if that is your choice (but it is definitely worth it if you pursue it!). You'll also be wise to secure an agent to pitch the book to publishers on your behalf. You will have to pitch the book, however, to secure the agent (I ended up with a great one), but we've already talked about pitching, so I know you can handle it. With so many publishing options available now, if writing a book is something on your bucket list, you should definitely go for it. I can't wait to read it!

Set Up Speaking Engagements

Another wonderful way to establish yourself as an authority is to book and participate in speaking engagements. Becoming a speaker is the gateway to establishing yourself as a supreme authority. It is a good method because you have a captive audience, are able to deliver precisely the message that you want to, and ultimately use it to sell yourself and book more gigs. You can schedule and arrange keynote presentations, retreats, workshops, and online webinars by reaching out to corporations and associations that are closely related to your areas of expertise (more pitching, but you are going to master that). Choose topics that are timely and relevant and will add value for your listeners. You should know your audience and fine-tune your message accordingly. I have delivered many different speeches on the topic of innovation, but each is different because I've tailored them according to the group I'm presenting to, such as CEOs or a sales team. You should keep the topics that you speak about narrow in relation to your expertise (the narrower the topic, the more likely you'll be viewed as an expert). It's a good idea to set up a speaker profile so that people can see what you speak about and learn a little more about you and your background.

When you are first starting out, you can set up your own panels, events, webinars, and more. It's a terrific way to get practice and create presentations that you can continue to use. You might even think about presenting for free (initially) for some companies and associations just to increase your exposure. Whether you'll work for free/exposure or not is a personal choice, but if you choose to do so, there can be some perks. For one, you should ask for a copy of the video recording so that you can use it as part of your media reel or put it on your site. A media reel is a video that brings together clips of you speaking and presenting (through live events, webinars, videos, etc.) and gives interested parties the opportunity to see what you are like onstage or on camera. I have one, and I rather like the way it turned out. You might also ask if the company or organization would give you a chance to sell your books or other products afterward by setting up a table at the back of the room. The experience can further be used as an opportunity to gather testimonials from audience members by recording their endorsements right on your phone—you can even get a microphone attachment for better sound quality. Testimonials are social proof of your speaking ability and are wonderful to include with your promotional mate-rials. You'll discover people are often excited to talk to you right after you've completed a presentation, so capitalize on that!

In general, you should also engage with your audience before and after your event. There are even speakers bureaus and professional speaking associations that you can join, including the National Speakers Association

(NSA), of which I am a member. There are others too, like Toastmasters, the Public Speakers Association, the Global Speakers Federation, and eSpeakers. You'll find that other members can help you network, and you can give and get referrals.

You might also try to arrange your own gigs by finding conferences, associations, and businesses related to your area of expertise or industry. After you've put together a list of prospects, create a pitch email or give the contact in charge a call. In your communication, introduce yourself (include a one-pager or brief summary about you), what you speak about, and how you can help them. Again, it's all about providing value. When conversing with the contact, try to find out exactly how you might help them solve a pain point and then further tailor your pitch and presentation. Work to build rapport and make a solid connection, and as with anything else related to selling, remember that it's a numbers game: the more people you reach out to, the more likely you'll be to book speaking engagements.

Speaking via live sessions on platforms like Instagram and Facebook is also a good way to go. They are increasingly popular and are a terrific place to hold Q & A sessions, training, and interviews and to give product demonstrations. Live sessions are a solid choice as you are able to interact with and respond to your audience in real time. Additionally, you can go live on YouTube and record videos there as well. When creating content on YouTube, be sure to look for commonly searched keywords and phrases related to your areas of expertise (you can use tools like TubeBuddy to help) and tailor your content accordingly. What's also nice about making YouTube videos is that you are able to easily share them on other platforms like LinkedIn, Twitter, and Facebook. We'll talk more about YouTube and the other platforms in the coming chapters. Overall, writing and speaking are excellent methods to share valuable, informative, and educational content to further position yourself as an expert and turn this Mindset Shift into a reality.

Start Podcasting

Podcasting is yet another method to establish yourself as a thought leader, network, and gain new prospects—all of which are important for a budding fempreneur. Think about your audience and who you are trying to attract. Knowing your audience can help you to develop a listener persona (similar to a customer persona, which we'll get into in more detail), an archetype for your target listener. Consider and identify the reasons that someone would want to listen to your podcast. What type of value will you provide, and why would people care? After that, list 15 or so possible podcast episodes that your audience might enjoy. Come up with a clever name and description too. Take care with selecting your episode titles as well; choose titles that are searchable and would appear in the results if someone was looking for information on the topic you're discussing. "How to" titles are popular, along with those that feature "tips." Ensure that the title showcases the value that the listener will get from tuning in.

Pay attention to your podcast length, too. What are others producing in the space? Do you want to do something similar in length because it's successful, or longer because it will give the audience something different? When it comes to releasing new episodes, try to be consistent. If you can only do one a month, stick with it. If you are able to commit to one a week, then do that. You can also arrange your podcasts in seasons as a method to organize and streamline them.

Another aspect to consider is whether your show will be solo, have a cohost, or feature guests—or maybe all of the above! You can also create and introduce an interview format, which provides a wonderful opportunity to network and bring exciting people on your show. Additionally, you might want to contemplate hosting a roundtable to incorporate multiple points of view.

It doesn't take much in terms of technology to get going. You must have a high-quality USB microphone and Internet access for starters. You will also need recording and editing software. Some types include Adobe Audition and Alitu, although there are many others. After that, you'll have to script and record your episodes. Try to avoid reading these scripts, as you want your podcast to sound conversational. Just pretend you're talking to your BFF! Also put a lot of care into the way that you open and close the episode. Consider adding music and cover art as well. You want to get listeners to stick with you and keep coming back for more. It is helpful to think of your broadcast like talking to someone right next to you. Be confident and personable and let your personality shine through. You are a successful fempreneur with a lot of knowledge to share with others!

Once you're done recording, you'll then have to edit your sessions using the software you've chosen. After you've gotten an episode edited the way you want, it's time to publish. For this, you'll need a host account, which can be obtained by signing up with a media hosting service. This service will host your audio files by setting up a spot on their site or putting them on your own website. After these steps have been taken, you can submit your podcast to different directories such as Spotify, Google Podcasts, and Apple Podcasts, where you'll attract listeners and hopefully new customers also. Sounds like fun, doesn't it? I'm hoping to launch my own podcast soon. You should too!

Create a Personal Website

All of the methods we've discussed come together to make it possible for you to be seen in the best light. Don't try to do everything we've talked about, however. You'll have to pick and choose. Remember, you can't do it all, but do what you can to grow your presence and establish yourself as an expert. As a final measure, pull your undertakings together by showcasing them on your website. I have my own site where I've included links to articles that I've contributed to; workshops and podcasts that I've hosted or participated in; and my books, videos, blog, and mentoring services. When people search for you, you want them to be able to find you and all of the things you've done to establish social proof and a strong brand. Having a carefully laid-out website will do just that, and if you're really serious about becoming a thought leader, it is entirely necessary.

Dream Big

I've become enamored with the idea of living every day as if you are interviewing for the opportunity of your dreams—the one that you don't know about yet or that maybe hasn't even been created. The reality is that people are sizing us up all of the time and taking mental notes about our skills and strengths. Our partners, clients, friends, and business acquaintances call upon those mental notes when an opportunity becomes available for something that we're good at. As such, we want to make sure that we're top of mind when that happens.

All of the methods that we've talked about are avenues that you can use to draw attention to your strengths, so put them out there. Assign yourself tasks that highlight the things that you enjoy and are passionate about.

Even if you aren't paid to do them, don't worry. The payment will come back to you eventually. There is always a way to integrate your passions into your career and business; you just have to get a little creative sometimes. The more you show what you know and love, the more likely it is to translate into eventual opportunities and revenue, so keep dreaming and pushing!

FINAL THOUGHTS

The fifth Mindset Shift will be critical to your journey as a fempreneur by lifting you to new heights through branding and building presence. It will take flight via your personal-branding strategy, which involves identifying your keywords, determining your value proposition, and crafting your elevator pitch. You'll take it to the next level through networking anywhere and everywhere you can: organizations; associations; social media; and online groups through LinkedIn, Facebook, and more. All the while, you'll be doing as much as you can to build visibility, particularly through thought leadership content: writing articles, blogging, making videos, contributing to media outlets, writing books, speaking, podcasting, and making appearances.

You have been shifting more and more into this entrepreneurial mindset and launching your inner entrepreneur. I have faith in you! As author and podcaster Brené Brown said, "Courage starts with showing up and letting ourselves be seen."[7] Go out there and let yourself be seen, fempreneur!

GETTING SOCIAL BY MASTERING SOCIAL MEDIA BASICS

Are you ready to get social? Oh, yeah! Since such a huge part of branding and building visibility today takes place on social media platforms, this chapter will guide you through the basics about the Mindset Shift that must occur for you to grow and maximize your social media presence and reach. This shift is very important for women entrepreneurs, because according to findings from a Finances Online study and Brandwatch, "females use social media less than men for business reasons. Generally, females use social networking sites to make connections and stay in touch with family or friends. Men, by contrast, use social media to gather the information they need to build influence. Social media helps them perform research, gather relevant contacts and ultimately increase their status."[1]

This chapter discusses methods for you to use as a fempreneur related to polishing overall brand style and presence while building engagement and followers; combating social media churn; dealing with negative comments or backlash online; maintaining overall quality and consistency of profiles, content, and feeds; and increasing engagement, brand reach, awareness, and number of followers. Mastering these areas is a critical aspect of this entrepreneurial Mindset Shift, and you must use them to get social and grow your business—one selfie or social media post at a time.

Consistency and Quality

There are so many reasons why branding and building presence on social media platforms is vital, but perhaps the main argument is that people are more likely to buy from a company or person they follow on social media. Other reasons include building brand awareness, boosting traffic, and creating community and dialogue with customers and potential customers. When it comes to your social media footprint, it's critical to focus on consistency. This consistency applies to your choice of colors (they should align with your brand personality), fonts, graphics and logos, and the frequency of your posts, too. An effective way to ensure that you are maintaining visual and content consistency is to establish a visual brand style guide. This style guide outlines all of these areas so that you are uniform across platforms and so you will create content that will appeal to your brand base and members of your target audience. It's like a little cheat sheet to ensure that you are staying on brand and that you can pass that social media quiz!

Design Your Logo

If you haven't already created a logo, this should be your first order of business. A logo is the symbol for your startup, and it will help your audience identify what you do and what you're about. It typically contains the name of your business along with some identifying marks and colors, and it should be reflective of your target audience and brand personality. Are you fun, young (define "young," you say), and cheerful? Or are you more serious and professional? Or somewhere in between (that's me)? Your logo design will show what your company is all about using wordmarks (business name only), brandmarks (image only), combination marks (business name and image), or lettermarks (initials only). In general, most logos showcase both their business name and relevant colors.

You can create your own logo, but I recommend getting a designer to help you as it will make your startup look more polished and professional. There are many graphic designers that you can hire on sites like Fiverr.com, a digital marketplace featuring freelance experts, fairly inexpensively. That's how I got my first logo. There were several iterations, but I eventually really loved what we came up with. Through the platform, you can check out previous work they've done to see if their style matches with your own. Then you will work with them to fine-tune a logo that you'll ultimately approve.

A logo lends to your brand personality and recognition and enables your target audience to identify your products and messaging with greater ease. It will be used on your website, packaging, social media sites, and more. Think of some logos that you would be able to spot anywhere, such as Apple's, Microsoft's, and McDonald's. I bet you start craving French fries when you see those golden arches—I know I do, and now I am! What is it about these logos that makes them so recognizable? How can you replicate that for your business, fempreneur?

Develop Your Visual Brand Style Guide

After you've established your logo, you'll next move on to creating your visual brand style guide. This guide provides instructions for everything associated with your brand, including information about colors and images and how you choose to showcase your brand externally on everything from your website down to your business cards. A visual brand style guide should include your company mission and values as well as information related to your logo and logo guidelines; this includes variations in color that are allowed, logo sizes, and the amount of clear space required around your logo. It should also outline the colors that can be used for your brand in their RGB (red, green, blue), CMYK (cyan, magenta, yellow, black), and Pantone variations and information related to your typography, such as font styles, size, and weight, all of which you can get from your designer (another reason to hire one). For example, one of the fonts for my logo is Rounded Elegance, and one of the colors I use is RGB #5cd4ef, CMYK 80,0,20,0.

Your visual brand style guide should also identify the guidelines for photos and graphics to be used (type, colors, etc.) and include keywords that describe the brand, attract your target audience, and exemplify your brand personality. An example of some keywords could be *fun, feminine, empowering,* and *energetic.* You can also add information about those things that your brand is not and what images, graphics, or colors would not represent the brand well. In this guide, there will be clear descriptions of suggested messaging that your customers can relate to. Ultimately, your visual brand style guide will direct you in making social media posts. As part of that, you'll want to ensure that the call to action for social media followers is well defined. The specifics of the call to action will likely vary depending on your marketing goals. Do you want to drive traffic to your site or get followers to make a purchase?

Describe Your Customer Personas

There may be multiple customer segments following you on each of the different platforms, so you'll need to map out which segments are associated with which platforms. It can be useful to create a customer persona for each segment so that you have a frame of reference when you are producing content. Think of a customer persona like a social media profile: it gives you insight into a person and is an archetype that is representative of a customer group or section of your target audience.

To put together a customer persona, assign a fictional name and photo that would represent someone in that segment—like Suzy Jones, weekend outdoor enthusiast; Joe Smith, young business professional; or Charlene Walters, kick-ass entrepreneurship mentor and crazed single mom!

Similarly, as I mentioned previously, you can craft a listener persona if you are launching a podcast. The one-page customer (or listener) persona will contain such demographic information as age, gender, race/ethnicity, needs/goals, relevant motivations and attitudes, related behaviors, frustrations/pain points with current products or services, level of expertise, environment, and how they are currently using the product or service. Also consider their challenges, fears, and marketing communication preferences.

Your customer persona should include a quote that encapsulates what these target customers might say that is indicative of their overall attitude and intent (in their own lingo/words). For example, for Suzy (above), "I work hard during the week, but I love to hit the trails on the weekend. I need hiking clothing and equipment that are comfortable, stylish, and durable and that make me look good while I'm climbing the trails."

You should group your customer personas by intent (you will have more than one persona per product), because there are different goals related to all customers, and grouping by intent is the best way to categorize them into segments. Your customer persona will also fine-tune your marketing messaging, including identifying keywords, marketing channels (social media, etc.), and the call to action for the customer (what action do you want this customer to take?). Giving your customer a name, quote, and intent is the entertaining part, so get really creative with it! If you are stumped by this process, it only means that you need to spend more time getting to know your customers and what drives them!

There are many benefits to developing customer personas, including personalization and properly addressing your customers' needs: the better you know and understand your audience, the better able you will be to reach and attract them. Be sure to look at your metrics and the data you've collected as well to further understand their behavior. What's more, creating a customer persona is fun, and you can derive a lot of joy from this activity. Why not bring together a group to work on it as a cool, bonding activity? Maybe host a girls' virtual luncheon with virtual lasagna? (There are no calories that way!)

Know Your Target Audience

It's important that your content entertains people, provides value, and is sharable and relatable. Part of this has to do with pinpointing your target market accurately and fine-tuning your messaging to them. A bit of this is review, but it's also an important aspect of your Mindset Shift, so it bears repeating.

You can determine your target audience by conducting thorough research. Look at your own customers if you already have them. If not, turn toward competitors and others in the industry. Who are their customers? What is their message? What would this group like more about your product or service? Or is there another similar group that would enjoy your products?

As part of this digging, you'll observe their demographic information, such as age, gender, race, occupation, location, income, and educational level. You should consider their psychographics as well, including personality, values, interests, hobbies, lifestyle, and behavior. Reflect on how your product or service will fit into your target market's lives and how they will use it.

The biggest mistake many new entrepreneurs make is defining their target market too broadly. Selling to "all women," or "men between 18 and 50 who have careers," is not narrow enough. A better example would be "men aged 25–40 who are single professionals interested in staying fit and active while living and working in the city." The reason you want to tighten it is so that you can better appropriate your brand messaging and budget to reach the people most likely to buy. You want to have your best shot at obtaining customers, don't you? You know it, girl!

There are other considerations as well. Ask key questions about whether there are enough people who fit into those parameters and if they will really benefit from the product. How many customers actually want a pink fireplace poker or a 30-pound lemon-scented air freshener? Is there a demonstrated need for the product, and do you thoroughly understand what will drive these customers to make a purchase decision? Can they afford to buy your product? What methods will you use to reach them, and where can you find them? Where do they congregate, both online and off?

Also consider the fact that more than one segment might be a good match for your product or service. For example, maybe your product was developed for one use, but an entirely different segment adopted it for another use; this often happens. Avon's Skin So Soft product is a good example: it was originally created as a skin moisturizer but found an even greater audience as a mosquito repellant. Now customers can have soft skin without any nasty bites—ahhh.

The better you have identified your target market and messaging, the more often your followers will share your content. The more engaged they are, the more likely you are to grow your base. It's also essential to sprinkle in some personality from time to time. Maybe you're super cool or a giant goofball like me. Whatever the case, roll with it. People want to get to know and be able to relate to you—so show that gorgeous face and inner beauty and intelligence in your content! The more they see you, the more they'll bond with your brand.

Another benefit of planning is your ability to automate content to ensure consistency with posts. You'll want to make sure that you are interacting and rewarding engagement and mentions, too. Engagement is a two-way street, so reciprocate! If you don't interact with others, they won't want to continue to interact with you.

Develop Your Social Media Content Strategy

You'll also have to come up with your content strategy. Begin by setting up your social media goals—they should be tied to your brand values and marketing plan. What are you hoping to achieve? If you want to convert more people from followers to customers, your objective might be to get them to go to your landing page. If you want to just increase your followers and brand awareness, it will be something else entirely.

Begin by using a tool, such as BuzzSummo or SpyFu (there are many others, too), to properly identify the keywords associated with your product and brand so that you can incorporate them into your messaging. You can also perform A/B tests on content to determine which posts are getting a higher level of engagement and interaction.

It is also useful to create a content schedule so that you can lay out how and when you'll be posting (as I mentioned previously). There are a number of scheduling tools that can help you, such as Buffer and Hootsuite. As with anything else, you'll have to check your metrics and see what is doing well and adjust accordingly. Lastly, you will need to promote certain posts, pins, and tweets to see which are the best at converting followers and customers and getting them to take other action.

It will also be essential to find ways to actively distribute your content so that you will broaden your reach. In fact, methods to expand your audience and get followers to share your content should be baked into your social media strategy. In order to effectively do so, align your brand's story-telling with what your audience is interested in. So, if you want to get your followers to buy your products, you must think of it in terms of being one step out from that: What is fun about choosing your product? What do your customers enjoy? Is it trying on new styles or imagining how they'll look in that sporty vehicle? Your interactions shouldn't be about asking them to buy directly but about connecting with them along points of the customer journey, nurturing the audience first before converting them to purchasers. So all of the content that you post should be customer-centric with that aim in mind. You can whip up a good story, can't you, girl?

Do a lot of research and see which platforms your target audience are on by digging in. There are many useful reports and data out there, such as the Facebook Audience Insights report. You will also need to figure out what they are doing on the platforms and what they like as well as what times they are engaging at the highest levels. Give people what they want, talk to them about what they are already saying and what they care about, all while pulling on their heartstrings from where they stand. You can best cater to your followers and tell the whole story by posting a variety of content that is tailored to these varied facets of the purchasing process and is entertaining while appealing to their emotions.

Think about driving traffic in terms of goals: awareness, reach, engagement, app installs, video views, lead generation, and so on. Each platform has built-in tools to help guide you when you are using marketing spend to achieve your goals, so utilize them and review the tutorials they provide to best understand them. You'll have to track certain key performance indicators at each stage to determine if you are hitting your benchmarks and tweak accordingly. Adjusting, pivoting, and being proactive are all part of the Mindset Shifts you've been making as a business owner, so they shouldn't be any problem for you to master in this regard.

Social Branding Trends

What you need to know about social media is that it always changes, but the desire for people to interact with each other will remain consistent. Let's discuss some current trends in social media that women entrepreneurs should leverage. These include focusing regularly on authenticity; using the power of humor; aligning your messaging with current events; and showcasing your charitable affiliations and social awareness. It will also be vital for you to use social listening and sentiment analysis to judge the success of your social media presence and to develop an understanding of what creates sticky conversation and long-term engagement instead of relying only on total followers. What's more, you must become savvy at using influencers (including micro-influencers and nano-influencers), creating dynamic ads that result in a more authentic connection with your audience, and leveraging employee testimonials and other user-generated content to grow your community.

Following and responding to social media trends (like those we'll discuss) is another crucial component of this Mindset Shift that is central to your success as a fempreneur! It's also really cool to watch trends and pivot, as I'm sure that you like to stay on top of the latest styles.

Be Authentic

Among the persistent trends in social media are a continuous focus on authenticity, the power of humor, and the ability to align with current events, as found in a recent Sprout Social study.[2] Being authentic on social media platforms is vital because authenticity builds trust. Consumers are naturally suspicious of marketing messages because they are being hit with so many all the time. We live in a world that's fraught with fake news and fake followers, so they are right to be skeptical. The challenge is to show the "real" side of your brand, and you can do this because you're up for a challenge and I'm sure that you don't like to be fake. Remember that two-faced friend you had at the office? Let's say "hell no" to being fake on social media, like you did to her!

Brand authenticity can be achieved by showcasing normal, day-to-day moments with customers and employees. Millennials in particular are drawn to authenticity, but the large majority of consumers are too, no matter the generation—some 86 percent, according to recent Social Media Week research.[3] That same research found that 91 percent of respondents said that they would be likely to reward brands that are authentic with a purchase or endorsement. That's huge, fempreneur!

You can project an image of authenticity by including pictures of yourself and employees to help build the connection between you and your followers. It's also helpful to be vulnerable and speak just as often about the things you've done wrong as you do about the things you've done right. Highlighting your customers and using their content as much as possible also furthers that authentic connection—it pulls them in, and other followers like to see that kind of content, too.

In general, as I've discussed before, the more you position yourself as trying to help instead of trying to make a "hard sale," the more likely your consumers will be to trust and bond with you, ultimately leading to those sales and endorsements. Attempting to push followers to buy immediately through your social media messaging is like putting plates of steak in front of your hard-core vegetarian friend and expecting her to eat them: save yourself the trouble!

A business that is successful and relevant on social media is one that functions as a storyteller, party enthusiast, and media mogul rolled into one. Call on your abilities in each of these roles, and invite your followers to the party, piquing their senses to elicit desired responses by serving them one morsel of marketing cake at a time. A study by Berger and Milkman found that posts that inspire high-energy emotions, such as enthusiasm and desire, are more likely to be shared, and that female authors had a higher chance of going viral than men![4] Awesome. Grab your keyboard and capitalize on your fempreneur strengths here.

Embrace the Power of Humor

Humor is another must-have in your social media repertoire. When you use comedy in your content, you get people's attention; being witty also helps customers remember you. Showing your funny side builds rapport with followers by appealing to them emotionally.

You do have to be careful with humor to avoid using anything that is "off-color" or potentially offensive; however, using a little wit, particularly on certain platforms, can go a long way. You know how you want to be around funny people—charming, witty, and oh-so-clever with those one-liners? The same is true with witty brands on social: we all need a little more to smile about in our days. Who doesn't love clever and pithy remarks?

Be sure your jokes fit your audience and that you use humor in a natural way. Even though business is serious, you can still find a way to infuse some lighter content. The funnier you are, the more likely your followers are to share the joke with their followers, and so on. Always consider if it's the right brand voice and tone for your audience so you will be less likely to potentially offend someone. You can even make a post funny just by using a humorous hashtag with an otherwise ordinary image and message. During the quarantine associated with the initial stages of COVID-19, I posted a picture of myself all dressed up with #AllDressedUpAndNoPlaceToGo. Everyone could relate to that sort of humor, as we were all trapped inside. Put the extra time in brainstorming here—it will really pay off.

When trying to come up with your punchlines, pay attention to trending topics, and look to YouTube and viral videos and content for inspiration. How were they able to successfully infuse humor into their content to make it resonate with their customers? You can even incorporate wit into your scheduling routine—by posting one funny piece of content per week, as an example. That humorous content can come in lots of forms, including memes, which many companies use as part of their posting strategy. This is something else that you can also try if it works well with your brand.

Strive to keep your funny posts unique—not something similar to what people have already seen a million times from other brands. Say "no way" to generic! Also, it's okay, and even a good idea, to make fun of yourself. We all love people who don't take themselves too seriously. What hilarious fact can you share about yourself that your followers can relate to? I'm sure that you have lots of them! I do. Did you burn your toast this morning or forget to pick up the one item that you set out to get at the store? (Hand raise over here!) We can all connect with these little mishaps.

Be Charitable

It's also impactful to showcase your charitable affiliations on social media and demonstrate that you are socially aware. Research has found that 83 percent of people in general are more likely to purchase a product with a social or environmental benefit and even more so for millennials (87 percent).[5] As such, it's important to find a cause to support and spotlight your charitability. It also helps with your marketing efforts and allows you to be seen as a brand that cares. I often volunteer with the United Service Organizations (USO) as well as another local charity and love to share and talk about it on social media. It raises awareness for the organizations, bringing their missions to life.

Broadcasting charitable activities on social platforms is a great idea because consumers prefer brands that support a charity that they care about, particularly during times of crisis, such as natural disasters and pandemics. It is also really helpful for raising brand awareness, as your brand will be showcased in the charity's social media feed. Further, 38 percent of millennials share positive information about companies and issues they care about online, and 30 percent of average consumers do as well—an added benefit.[6]

As the head of a startup, you can share your success by giving products, funds, and volunteer hours to worthy causes and then posting about it. Try to pick a nonprofit that aligns with your business offerings, target audience, and values. Many charitable organizations need financial support to achieve their objectives, and giving to these nonprofits and charities is a good thing to do while positioning your company in a favorable light in the eyes of others.

Don't Rely on Vanity Metrics

Marketers are moving away from judging the success of their social media presence by using vanity metrics, such as the number of followers and "likes." Instead, there has been more of a focus on social listening and sentiment analysis, according to Sprout Social research.[7] This is partly a result of major platforms experimenting with removing "likes" in response to outcries that vanity metrics are causing some addictive and unhealthy behaviors on social. Who needs all those "likes" anyhow?

It's now about *what* is being said instead of *how many*—brands must focus more on long-term engagement or what's making the conversation sticky. It's also about an increased emphasis on return on investment (ROI) for paid and boosted posts and tweets. It's easier than ever before to track ROI because we can get more insight into our followers' activities online. For example, you can see if they were compelled enough by one of your posts or ads to buy a product or visit your landing page. Your non-paid social media strategy should still focus on overall brand engagement and community building.

Instead of "likes" and follower counts, the metrics that are becoming more meaningful include view duration, view-through rate, or click-through rates. Some cutting-edge companies are even using facial recognition technology to judge people's reactions to social media posts and content—isn't that cool? A report from Red Sky Predictions goes so far as to forecast the complete disappearance of vanity metrics.[8] In general, as a business owner, you will have to look more closely at lead generation and lead conversion to measure the effectiveness of your campaigns, particularly those that involve social media spend.

Use Dynamic Ads

With all of the social media platforms, you can focus your ads at a certain target audience based on their location, age, gender, and past buying habits. This kind of laser-focused advertising is not only available; it's also now the norm. We are no longer strategizing for the widest reach but the most specific reach, and particularly prevalent is the increased use of dynamic ads.

Dynamic ads are basically banners that change to adapt to each user with more targeted content, tailored precisely to him or her automatically. I bet you've been hit with them before, and in some cases were probably totally spooked out by their accuracy. Did they read your mind?

To create one for your brand, you'll need to upload a digital file that contains all of your product information, called a product feed, and use an ad delivery solution, like Facebook's, that customizes it in real time to deliver the most applicable landing page to each user. The process of using dynamic ads helps marketers (like you) to use data such as browsing history, geolocation, and behavioral information to select the right ad to match with the user's preferences and needs—all done behind the scenes.

With their narrow focus, dynamic ads increase ROI and decrease marketing costs. They also boost loyalty, allow you to deliver ads that are relevant to each user, and enable you to target customers who have visited your website and looked at your products but bounced before making a purchase. This is an already interested audience that you want to try to convert.

To help set up these ads, you can, for example, insert a Facebook pixel on your site—it's a snippet of code that tracks the actions that people take on your website, including which products they've looked at or placed in a cart. You can also set up a product feed in which you supply all the necessary information—such as product descriptions, sizes, price, shipping, images—and create dynamic ads in Google Ads as well. It's clear why dynamic ads continue to be the preferred method to gain customers and conversions, and they should certainly be part of your customer acquisition strategy as a savvy female business owner.

Leverage Influencers

Positive recommendations from trusted sources, or influencers, can do so much for your brand. According to the Digital Marketing Institute, 49 percent of consumers rely on influencer recommendations.[9] That's big! Sprout Social research found that while brands are still relying on influencers, there has been a shift toward using more micro-influencers (accounts with

1,000 to 10,000 followers) and nano-influencers (accounts with fewer than 1,000 followers) who have a more authentic connection with their audience.[10] There has also been more of a call for influencers to back up their numbers with data and authenticity. Again, we see a push toward engagement and away from total number of followers.

Influencers today include writers, bloggers, podcasters, and those with substantial, loyal social media followings. These influencers are the prom kings and queens of social media—like that person in high school who wore a red T-shirt one day and then five more people showed up in school the next day wearing the same red shirt!

So how do you identify which influencers you might work with or who would be a good match for your company? Look to industry hashtags, blogs, articles, and podcasts to target influencers whose following aligns with your target audience, who are active in your industry, and who fit well with your brand. Next, check to see how aligned and relevant their content is to your messaging, how engaged their audience is, what their reach is like, how frequently they will be able to recommend your product or service, and if they are authentic and have a solid relationship with their followers.

After you find some potential influencers, give some thought to the type of content that you want them to share, as well as guidelines for sharing and the measures you'll use to determine the effectiveness of their endorsements. You might want to experiment with using influencers to determine how effective it is for achieving your marketing goals until you fine-tune the exact recipe or decide that it is not the right avenue for you.

Influencer marketing, in the correct form, can be a good strategy for you as a new business owner. In the words of Malorie Lucich, head of marketing communications at Pinterest, "People share, read, and generally engage more with any type of content when it's surfaced through friends and people they know and trust."[11]

Build a Community

Today, consumers want to feel that they are more than just customers—they want to be part of something bigger (don't you?) and bond with a brand on a deeper level, establishing a relationship with them online. They want you to be their BFF, Sherpa, and cheerleader all in one, so take steps to make your target audience snuggle up to your company.

As a female founder, you will do well to continue to focus on growing your community by leveraging employee testimonials and other user-generated content. Some brands that have a notably strong social media presence and community are Wendy's, Progressive, and NorthFace, to name just a few; there are many out there. I applaud Wendy's for its use of pithy replies on social media and its ability to spar with competitors. It's hysterical how Wendy's tells Burger King and McDonald's where to go. Progressive has really given a friendly face to its social through the use of its characters Flo and Jamie: who doesn't get a kick out of Flo and Jamie and their misadventures? And NorthFace's use of inspirational images and focus on "disconnecting," along with engaging its followers and building its community, makes it a standout on social. NorthFace's ads certainly make me want to climb a mountain! Is there any doubt what these brands are about?

Think about your brand personality (you're awesome!) and customers, and how you can get them to relate to and rally around your startup. How might you pull them into the conversation and compel them to share their experiences, their joys, and their everyday lives with you? You can do so in many ways, so flex your creative muscles here, ladies.

For starters, tag your customers and invite them to post videos and photos engaging with your products, initiate challenges, use community hashtags, and offer promotions and giveaways. These community-building activities often foster subscriptions and repeat business, and they enable your followers to establish authentic relationships with each other (through shared interests and goals), which is even more valuable and further establishes their relationship with your brand. Many businesses go so far as to create groups and fan pages to take this bonding to an even greater level! So, create and capitalize on your community, and take advantage of the other trends we've discussed as part of this sixth Mindset Shift, fempreneur!

Monitoring Social Media Churn

Once women entrepreneurs have their social media up and growing, it's important for us to also monitor social media churn—the percentage of followers lost over time—across all of our platforms. As a startup founder, you must begin to understand how to reduce social media follower churn by interacting regularly with your audience and confirming that you are adding value to your followers' lives.

Some strategies for doing so include being responsive to your followers' posts and comments; getting your audience involved through serving up opportunities to share their own content; running contests that followers can participate in; analyzing and adjusting your social content based on what resonates most with your target audience; finding new and engaging ways to deliver your messages; and taking corrective measures if something happens that damages your company's reputation. Let's dig in further, fempreneurs.

A recent study by GoodFirms found that the main reasons that people unfollow brands on social media include bad customer service; content that's not applicable; too much promotion; talking about politics or controversial social issues; posting too often; and a lack of engagement or ignoring followers' comments, posts, and mentions (eek—breaking the golden rule of social media!).[12] Think about your own experience. Have you unfollowed any people or brands for these reasons? Those who follow you are no different.

Reducing social media follower churn is not as elusive as it may sound, and some simple ways to do so begin with engaging with followers frequently and providing valuable, interesting, and entertaining content— poke, evoke, and joke. You should, at a minimum, engage with those who are engaging with you. Nobody likes a one-sided conversation, so reciprocity should be at the heart of all of your social media activities. Heck, it's a lot of fun too.

It pays to get proactive and interact on your loyal followers' feeds as well, follow them back, and repost and share their content when applicable. Pull your audience in by posting challenges and inviting them to share content related to your brand. You want them to be so close to the brand that they're stuck like a Band-Aid. You can also host contests and promotions that will drive engagement, such as agreeing to send free samples to the first 50 people who comment on your posts or tagging loyal followers who you think may relate to your content. These practices and others will up the level of interaction with your brand and make fun and entertainment central to the equation. Put simply: to build community on social, you should show love, invite fun, and make your followers smile!

If you are dealing with decreasing followers on your social media page (oh, drat!), come up with a new strategy. Ask questions, evaluate metrics, and ascertain why they are unfollowing you. Analyze which content is resonating more with your target audience and adjust accordingly, continuing to up the ante and find new and appealing ways to deliver your messages.

Additionally, if something happens that damages your company's reputation, the best corrective measures are to own up to the problem, apologize if it was offensive, and make restitution in a way that will be appreciated by those who were offended. Simply show your audience and customers that you're sorry. It's also best to avoid the urge to delete negative comments; address them instead. You should always respond to and not avoid undesirable scenarios—your audience will respect you more for it. Recognizing and addressing social media churn and problems is the last part of this Mindset Shift as a fempreneur, so make it a part of your ongoing business practices. Don't let them go quietly!

FINAL THOUGHTS

You are now fluent in each of the three main aspects of this entrepreneurial Mindset Shift: focusing on consistency and quality, staying abreast of social media trends, and monitoring and correcting social media churn. So speak the language, because you've got it down, girl, and have now mastered these social media musts.

I'll close with this: just be yourself on social platforms, and remember that it takes a village—so do what you can to educate, inspire, embolden, and cheer others on. Lift up your community by understanding that everyone is a VIP member and that you are the hostess who is responsible for the *ultimate experience*, serving up gobs of value, miles of smiles, and oceans of good cheer. It wouldn't be a party without you!

STAYING SOCIAL BY LEVERAGING SOCIAL MEDIA OPTIONS

Now that you've mastered the basics, are you ready to stay social by leveraging your social media platforms? Buckle up because there's more to learn in Mindset Shift 7, and this knowledge is important to your fempreneurial success. A recent study by the Digital Branding Institute found that in terms of social media branding, "men are more aggressive [than women] and like to use social media for researching their competition and growing their networks."[1] We'll continue the discussion of the Mindset Shift that's required of women entrepreneurs in branding and building presence via social media by delving into several options for individual platforms: Instagram, Twitter, LinkedIn, Facebook, TikTok, Snapchat, Pinterest, and YouTube. It's time to get you posting, snapping, tweeting, pinning, and going live!

Instagram

Let's begin with a discussion of Instagram. Every platform is different, and given Instagram's surging popularity, you will want to get this one right.

Create a Compelling Bio

When setting up your Instagram profile, start with your bio, which is the first impression potential followers will get of your business. When creating it, choose your description and keywords with care, and put some thought into your call to action. Do you want your followers to visit your website, download an article, or make a purchase? Direct them and provide a link so that they can take that action. Followers and potential followers should get a good idea of who you are and what your business does. Your bio is also the place where you have the opportunity to showcase important clients and achievements and use emojis that enhance and organize your information.

Select the profile picture or logo for your brand with care, focusing on image quality and ensuring that it's consistent with all of your other social media platforms. Your fans and followers should be able to easily locate you no matter what platform they're on, and aligning your profile pictures and images will make it easier for them to do so. I have the same profile picture and username on all of my platforms so that I can be quickly found and followed (and as an author and mentor, I am the brand)! I go by Charlene Walters, PhD, because there are a ton of Charlene Walters out there, but only one Charlene Walters, PhD (okay, maybe there are more, but they are not as active on social).

Consider Aesthetics for Maximum Visual Appeal

Instagram is a highly visual platform, so pick strong photos and videos to post. It helps to hire a photographer and get many different images that you can use moving forward—pictures of your products, employees, customers, and you! You can utilize these photos to create custom graphics with an app, enabling you to add personalized messaging and logos. The app that I often use is called PostMuse, but there are lots of them out there. If you're on a tighter budget—and as we've talked about, saving money is a great idea when you're just starting out—you can use stock photos and search by color to keep them consistent with your brand style.

Choose fonts and colors that are harmonious with your visual brand style guide—either several key colors or a more monotone approach and one or two font choices. You should also try to select a theme, which will vary depending on your business. Do you want an elegant look? More playful or organic? Be consistent with your selected theme as well as your filter and border choices: they should be uniform. A repetitive border can really give your photos a professional, aligned look, particularly if you like to post a variety of images, as I do.

Take care with your overall Instagram aesthetic—remember that it should showcase your brand personality and what you want to convey—so select image and filter choices thoughtfully to result in a look that's solid and cohesive. In terms of engagement, some of the most popular filters on Instagram (according to an Iconosquare study) are No Filter, Clarendon, Juno, Lark, and Ludwig—this can vary depending on your audience.[2] I tend to prefer No Filter and Juno; how about you?

Instagram users decide whether or not to follow you very quickly while scrolling through your feed. That means everything you post must work together and be appealing to the eyes—think sexy, attractive, interesting, and compelling here (like that gorgeous guy or girl at the gym that you used to try to get the treadmill next to). Make sure that you are showing your followers what they are looking for while still infusing your brand into your content—it's possible and even a good idea to work on your layout before you post—by using a mood board (a collage of images and objects) to brainstorm and see how certain colors and styles work together or by previewing content using a preview app. I post a picture of myself at least every third photo to consistently put myself in my Insta mix, since I am the brand as a thought leader. The look that you pull together will give a strong impression of your business, and people will decide whether or not to follow you based on that. You want people—lots of people—to follow you, right?

Choose Your Content Wisely

If you are unsure about what to post, look to others in your industry and research the type of content they are sharing—consider this additional market research friendly spying and yourself Nancy Drew or Veronica Mars. When determining what to put out there, keep adding value through educational or inspirational posts, promotion, and creating connections to remain top of mind. Make them laugh, make them cry, take them away from their dirty dishes and regrets, and pull them into your story.

You should also pick three to four key topics to focus on so that your content is not all over the place. Infuse your company culture and story throughout, and piggyback on trending topics, holidays, and recent news. You can also use the platform to promote giveaways and special offers. Why not send some free SWAG to the 100th person who comments, for instance? Keep it conversational (use your audience's lingo and fun slang) and have a call to action like "tag someone who'd like this," "see what's in our newsletter," or "sign up for our weekly blog." Make your followers a part of the story, girl.

Don't Forget About Text

Although Instagram is highly visual, captions here increase engagement, so take advantage and use them—long or short—so that your content tells a story with emotions. A picture is worth 1,000 words, of course, but words count for word count, too! Many even use their Instagram feed as a blog, which is a possibility for you as well. Invite your followers in on the fun: when you tag them, you are enticing them to come along for the experience, and they will be flattered and more loyal to you. Also, you will create a viral effect as they share and invite their friends to join in on the conversation, so tag away, fempreneur!

Schedule Your Posts

Once you've begun to identify and create content, you'll delve into scheduling, and there are several scheduling tools available to help you, including Hootsuite, Buffer, and Sprout Social. Pay attention to your frequency and timing, and post consistently when your users are most active. How often to post will depend on your followers: do they get up early for a morning run (checking their social before they go), or are they night owls who scroll into the wee hours of the night? Experiment a little and give them time to engage before posting more content; otherwise, they might become overwhelmed and miss some of your posts.

Be consistent, but avoid posting at a fixed time, as that will make your brand look a little more robotic and less personal. You're no robot, fempreneur, but I'm sure you feel like Wonder Woman sometimes (and you totally are). Scheduling posts ahead of time is helpful because it allows you to plan your content a month or two in advance and ensures the frequency we've been talking about, taking day-to-day posting off of your already full entrepreneurial plate!

Push Engagement—Without Being Pushy

Once you get your branding and posting schedule down, you'll next turn your focus toward increasing engagement and gaining new followers through interaction. Leveraging hashtags is one strategy for doing so. Use popular hashtags as well as those that are branded for your business; research the ones that are trending and most used or followed in your industry and take advantage of their power to broaden your reach. Hit return a few times after adding hashtags to your post to create a less-cluttered look, or opt to include your hashtags in the first comment instead to thwart negative algorithmic consequences while also preventing your post from appearing spammy.

You can find popular hashtags by using tools like Websta or Iconosquare, and follow them—choose between 15 and 20 related hashtags for every product you sell. Keep in mind that the most popular are not always ideal, as your posts can get lost, so use a variety, and interact with people who follow and post under these hashtags, too. After all, there are only certain groups of people who will follow hashtags like #lifeenthusiast or #ilovebees, and depending on your target market, these might be your people! #youvegotthis

Look at your competitors and engage with their followers as well by following those users who are in your target audience; you can also like and comment on their photos. Again, more friendly espionage! A combination of these three methods—following, liking, and commenting—will yield the highest follow-back rate, and don't be afraid to ask for more followers either, by using sponsored ads.

Consider Insta Influencers

You can also leverage influencer marketing on Instagram. Try to find those people with anywhere between 20,000 and 200,000 followers to help promote your brand. But don't disregard micro- and nano-influencers either, as they often have a more genuine connection with their audience (as we've discussed previously). You can pay them for sponsored ads or product reviews. When in doubt, DM them and ask about their sponsored pricing. When choosing whom to contact, be sure that you are not looking solely at their number of followers but also their engagement.

Remember to reciprocate: when an influencer engages with you, engage back. It's also good to team up with other people who may be similarly poised. You can feature them in your posts, blogs, and podcasts, and then broadcast it on Insta. They'll be flattered and will often repay the favor. You can even create and join pods—collective groups of Instagrammers—to support each other in terms of engagement. This practice boosts how often your posts appear and nudges the Instagram algorithm in your favor. I am a member of several such unofficial pods and find them to be very helpful—this goes back to reciprocity and supporting others, which is important in life and business—so get your girl gang together.

Add Stories

Be sure to use Instagram stories, a feature within the app where users can share videos and images in a slideshow format. They are a great way to briefly highlight moments and happenings, and they give you a lot of opportunity to interact with followers. They are only gaining in popularity, too. Stories are a creative method to serve up additional content without overwhelming your followers. Organize your stories into highlights, providing your followers with an enhanced idea of what your brand stands for and establishing themes on your bio. Stories are a nice area to post short videos and use swipe-up links to promote products, although in order to do so, you'll need at least 10,000 followers. Don't fret, you'll get there.

Measure Metrics

Finally, track your followers and engagement closely—there are plenty of apps and analytics tools that will help you to do so. Look at lost followers, most-engaged followers, least-engaged followers, admirers, ghost followers, and stalkers, and try to engage or reengage with those who fall into these categories. Watch for trends and patterns (it's really interesting, too—checking out the ones who are checking you out, or not). You'll also want to closely monitor the content that most resonated with your target audience to note engagement while using this data to inform your content strategy moving forward.

In closing, food writer and entrepreneur Ella Woodward of Deliciously Ella said, "I'm on my phone 24/7, replying to every Instagram comment and message to try to understand how people are seeing us, and their questions and concerns."[3] Follow Ella's lead, fempreneurs, in getting to know, engaging with, and being responsive to your customers on Insta. I am also right there doing this every day, with her and now you!

Twitter

Let's talk about Twitter next. Tweet. Tweet. Twitter has a whole different flavor and feel than Instagram—here, it's about the conversation. With more than 321 million active monthly users, it's hard to ignore this powerhouse platform.

Create Your Bio and Pinned Tweet

Similar to Instagram, you will start by fine-tuning your bio, making sure you have a professional image and banner that is consistent with your other social media profiles and including information that highlights your company's successes, achievements, and high-profile clients or affiliations. Include a link to your website or blog, too.

Also, pay attention to your pinned tweet, which should reflect your business and brand; change it out frequently to keep it fresh. I typically include a pinned tweet to an article about my mentoring services or to recent pieces that I've written or been featured in—for instance, when I was cited as one of 150 Marketers to Follow (so cool).

Set Your Strategy

As with anything else, you must come up with your Twitter strategy, deciding what you want to focus on. Generally speaking, you'll be concentrating on brand awareness across all platforms, but you will probably look at other areas as well, such as customer acquisition, app installs, website clicks, growing followers, or customer engagement, perhaps. Set goals for yourself. Maybe you want to gain 100 new customers per month or get a certain number of followers to subscribe to your newsletter. Think strategically, fempreneur!

Next, you'll need to decide on your content strategy. Use this platform to generate conversations, educate, entertain, or share ideas, using tweets that are short and highly focused. There are different types of content that you can tweet. For example, you can share your blog posts, promos, news about your company, articles, videos, shout-outs, employee or company photos, and short relevant comments. You can also center some of your content around holidays, motivational quotes, upcoming events, or trending topics and recent news, which make your posts feel current.

Hashtags on Twitter double the amount of engagement with your tweets—I have certainly found this to be the case with mine. Look for trending hashtags, and post when there is the most activity—usually between 9 and 10 a.m. on weekdays, but this can vary depending on your audience. Try to post at least once a day, but since it's such a busy site, two to three times a day is ideal. You want to project the appearance that you are always active. So post consistently, but not at fixed times, as you don't want to seem artificial.

As with everything else, you'll want to engage and track engagement—it's a two-way street. Remember that you are driving conversation, so retweet, mention, ask questions, interact, and show that you care about your followers. Think about your voice and use humor when you can, as Twitter is probably the most ideal of all the platforms for using wit. As model and influencer Gigi Hadid said, "Twitter is the place where I try to be more funny. And then I use Instagram just as my diary. I pull [off] some jokes on there, but I think people have a better sense of humor on Twitter."[4] She's right: it is an excellent platform for showing your witty side, so embrace it like Gigi does!

Revisit your brand personality, and don't shy away from using pictures, videos, and gifs on Twitter, since they work well there. One of my favorites is Alfonso Ribeiro doing the Carlton Dance. (Who doesn't love Carlton's moves?) Overall, keep your content diverse on different platforms—it should be related but unique at the same time. Don't post the same post on Facebook, Instagram, and Twitter (yawn!), because each of these platforms has a different vibe. So mix it up, keep it human, and showcase your brand personality, always reciprocating and being responsive.

Consider Using Promoted Tweets

When you are a little further along with your entrepreneurial journey, you may want to invest in promoted tweets or Twitter ads. You might even consider using Promote Mode, which does much of the heavy lifting for you. When deciding on promoted tweets, reflect upon your goals, budget, and target audience, and stay away from any content that will get viewers to click away from your ad, like hashtags or mentions. When you are mentioned, however, be sure to retweet it— after all, that's additional content, and you want to reward that type of follower behavior. Follow the leader, leader! Follow the leader!

Grow Your Audience

Once you've got your content strategy and schedule down, you should turn your focus to expanding your audience. You can do so in several ways, including leveraging other feeds and mentioning and interacting with brands and influencers. Include your Twitter handle on the bottom of your email signature, embed your Twitter feed on your website, and use Twitter buttons on both your blog and website. No matter what, resist the urge to purchase fake followers, as it will become pretty clear to others that they are not real users, and there will be little engagement, leaving a negative impression. You want real followers because real followers buy; fake ones don't—they only have fake money!

Don't be above participating in Follow Fridays or Self-Promo Saturdays and joining Twitter communities that are related to your area of expertise. There are several other methods that you can use to grow your audience, too, including following people, and liking and commenting on their tweets—a combination of these three should yield the best results. Pull more people into your feed by tagging other brands and accounts, looking at your competitors and interacting with their followers, monitoring keywords in the industry, live tweeting at events, providing pictures and updates, and asking questions that will engage your followers.

Use Lists

Another great strategy on Twitter is to use Lists, which is also an awesome way to categorize your followers and keep track of and target content. First, give the list a name, then choose people and companies to include. Ensure that the names you choose for the lists are complimentary, as the people that you add will be notified that you've added them. So avoid names like "Whiners" or "Bores" (even if that's what you think)! You should also subscribe to other people's lists as well: it's a good way to build community.

Contemplate Other Strategies

If you use videos on Twitter, you are much more likely to be retweeted. When in doubt about your posts, you can always utilize an A/B test and see which tweets resonate more with your audience. Also, be sure to share versus constantly self-promoting, as we've already established that people don't want to be pitched at all the time; they want to be entertained and informed (think *yeah, yeah, yeah!* instead of *blah, blah, blah*).

Write well and have someone look over your tweets before you post them, too. There is no edit button on Twitter, so be forewarned! I can't tell you how many times I've noticed a typo after the fact, so check and double check before you tweet. It's a good practice to always maintain a personal Twitter account, too, so you can interact with brands from a consumer's perspective, and you can also utilize Twitter Live, a live video streaming feature, to livestream.

Leverage Influencers

On Twitter, as with other platforms, you should try to engage with and use influencers. These are the people who tweet about products similar to yours, your competitors, or your industry in general. There are certain tools (like FollowerWonk and BuzzSumo) that you can use to find them by entering relevant keywords, but before deciding to work with any particular influencer, look at their follower base, mentions, and social shares to ensure that they are a good fit with your business. Then engage with them, ask them industry questions, and watch their interactions, making sure that you notice and connect with the ones who've shown interest in you through their likes and retweets, and work to continue the relationship—even providing incentives when so inclined.

You'll want to track everything on Twitter through Twitter analytics and other Twitter analysis apps. Analyze followers, impressions, total engagements, likes, detail expands, retweets, replies, hashtag clicks, and profile clicks, and adjust accordingly to maximize your presence and reach. I've had so many pleasant interactions on Twitter and have made a lot of solid connections there. It's also kind of amazing when you see your Twitter notifications blow up and wonder what sort of conversations you've been looped into. Go forth and tweet your heart out, girl—you've got this Twitter thing!

LinkedIn

Let's look at LinkedIn next. This platform is considered the nerd of social media (compared to its cooler cousins, Instagram and Twitter), but it's the most important one for networking and growing your business.

Create Your Personal Profile

When it comes to LinkedIn, we are going to tackle it from a two-pronged approach. As an entrepreneur, you'll have to establish and maintain both a personal profile and a business page. This platform is arguably the best for networking and expanding your circle, and your first order of business will be to set up your profile. As you do so, pay heed to personal branding tactics that will further your opportunities and visibility and make you stand out from others.

To begin, select a picture and cover photo that project professionalism and confidence. Take time with your summary to highlight your strengths, expertise, and abilities, then fill in your education and skills. Choose your headline, a description of you that is 120 characters or less, with the same care as when you craft anything else, avoiding headlines that are overly cheesy or salesy. Refrain from listing your main job title as your headline if you are a side hustler; instead, emphasize titles that feature your expertise and areas that you want to be known for, as well as your business. This portion is all about *you*, wonderful, glorious *you*, and is doubly important if you're a solopreneur.

Set Up Your Business Page

Next, you'll set up a business page for your brand. This is the place to highlight your company. In the "About Us" section, you have 2,000 characters to describe what your startup does and why people should be interested. Be sure to incorporate your keywords, put an emphasis on brand voice, and include your URL and other important information. The good news with LinkedIn is that you can also create Showcase Pages, where you can emphasize your services, products, divisions, and more, enabling you to tailor information more precisely. Post to these pages a lot to keep them fresh, and include employees and their testimonials if you are a larger company.

LinkedIn is also a good place to leverage endorsements, so you should both collect and give endorsements from relevant parties, such as employees, clients, and coworkers (remember, if you don't ask, you don't get). Stay on top of what's happening on this platform by watching your competitors and paying attention to LinkedIn's 10 best company pages to see what they are doing that you might be able to replicate. Your competitors are checking you out—believe me! It happens to me all the time. If you have a slightly more established business, you can encourage your employees to connect and interact on the business pages, too.

Grow Your Presence

Similar to other platforms, you'll want to grow your LinkedIn presence. One of the surest ways to accomplish that is by being particular about the content you are posting. According to LinkedIn recommendations, you should be posting once per weekday. This may seem like a lot when you're first starting out, so perhaps begin by posting once a week and grow from there. I personally believe that is more than sufficient.

LinkedIn is an excellent place to share your own blogs or articles (and you should), and other videos and content from noteworthy news sources as well. With LinkedIn Publishing, you can create your own content right there on the platform, too. If you post with images, you'll get more comments and interaction—I've seen this time and time again—so include them whenever possible.

Be certain to also take advantage of LinkedIn groups, as again, LinkedIn is the best platform for networking, and these groups are a wonderful place for you to connect with other thought leaders, influencers, and experts in your field, as well as to forge professional connections. Join groups that align with your interests and business goals, and once in them, interact and participate in discussions regularly. These interactions and activities will bring people to your company page and get them to visit your profile; you'll gain customers, advocates, and possible strategic partnerships as a result.

As you gain traction, you can also consider using LinkedIn ads. There are several types. One is sponsored content, which can be useful in getting people to visit your business page. Another is text or pay-per-click ads, which can appear in groups, on homepages, search results, or group and profile pages. Lastly, you can send sponsored InMail, which goes directly to user's inboxes when they are active on LinkedIn, which makes your messages more likely to be seen and read (which you want).

Track It

As with other types of social media, you must track everything and can do so using LinkedIn analytics. On your business page, you are able to track visitors, updates, and followers. You can also check interactions with your posts, including views, engagement, and information about who's looking, where they work, and where they're geographically located.

Like I mentioned before, LinkedIn is all about connecting and allowing people to find you—it's a place to brag professionally and make friends who inspire and motivate you. Ensure that your personal profile is always updated and very professional, and then interact and connect continuously.

It's best practice to send personalized notes when connecting with new people on LinkedIn, and I've even known people who send out individualized videos to all new connections—which is time-consuming but a nice personal touch. Be sure to leverage LinkedIn stories too. The same as with the other platforms, interaction is a two-way street, so engage and join groups and participate in discussions. In other words, provide value and you'll get value back. If you engage actively on LinkedIn, you're saying "Hey world—check me out" without actually using the words. So, check you out, girl! You're going to make the most of LinkedIn!

Facebook

Next, let's touch on Facebook—the fairy godmother of platforms. Although it seems like it's been around forever, Facebook still remains a social media leader due to its large user base: it currently has more than 2.5 billion users, and it's still growing.[5] It's also popular because of its ability to track users by location, demographics, and interests, and when using Facebook, companies can set up brand and product pages, fan pages, and more. The Facebook algorithms can be attractive to many businesses, but they are always changing depending on Facebook's emphasis at the moment. Facebook controls how much of your content is seen and by whom, so you have to adjust constantly. Ultimately, Facebook's goal is to increase its own paid advertising, so keep that in mind.

Facebook may seem a bit passé in terms of social media appeal, but it is still relevant because it remains an important force as a mass media channel. Consider creating a Facebook fan page for your brand, product, company, and more. Because Facebook's algorithm, which is based on key ranking signals, is so often adjusted, you are somewhat at the mercy of the platform regarding your exposure, but this is true of other social media platforms as well. When organic reach is down on Facebook, the company is trying to drive more paid advertising. Whatever tweaks and changes Facebook makes will always have a major impact on how and if users will see your content. On the positive side, this platform can enable more accuracy, with targeted content allowing it to appear in the newsfeeds of more users who are interested in your products and services, which helps with brand awareness and growing your customer base. Another positive associated with Facebook is that it is also a platform that is very conducive to sharing and interaction with likes, loves, cares, and wows!

Set Up Your Business Page

When using Facebook, the first thing you should do is set up your business page. Begin by identifying which category your business falls into and then choosing images for the page. Select visuals that clearly reflect your brand (if in doubt, refer back to your brand style guide). Your cover photo and profile image should accurately demonstrate both your brand personality and style. And, once again, your username should be as consistent as possible across platforms.

With these formalities out of the way, you'll next add your company information, similar to what we've discussed for other social media outlets. Your description and categories here are important, as well as your contact details, location, and hours. Your page provides another chance for you to showcase your brand story, so spin an amazing tale!

Solidify Your Strategy

Next, you must outline your content strategy for Facebook, create and schedule your posts, and then invite people to like your page. The highest level of interaction on Facebook tends to occur during the middle of the week (Tuesday–Thursday), usually between 10 a.m. and 3 p.m., according to a recent Sprout Social study.[6] To be successful on Facebook, include content that starts conversations, and understand that recency is important when it comes to the ranking algorithms—so post when your users are online. Also, avoid racy or politically charged content or anything that is linked to an iffy website or identified as fake news. Facebook is a great spot to post videos that are at least three minutes in length: these videos will get more engagement compared to text posts, and they will be ranked higher. Posting frequently helps increase your value with followers and, again, helps with your ranking.

When choosing what type of content to post on Facebook, use strategies similar to those we've discussed for other social media. Consider your brand voice and target audience and what might resonate with them, and be sure to inform, educate, inspire, and entertain. Spotlight company events, awards, outings, employees, and customers, and show your personality, while always engaging with your Facebook fans. Aim to post content that will motivate others to share and ignite discussions, like, and comment frequently to convert your followers into raving brand ambassadors, and use pictures to showcase your products, services, and customers.

Final Facebook suggestions: don't miss the opportunity to add compelling content, post stories, and always use hooks to draw your followers to take action—yank on their heartstrings, plead to their wallets, and make their souls sing!

As with all platforms, you must track your analytics. Look at Page Insights, where you can follow such metrics as post reach, page views, page likes, and more. You can also use your Facebook page to drive traffic to your website and to boost your SEO (search engine optimization).

Elevate your Facebook page with a call to action, have a pinned post, invite your Facebook friends to take action in all of your posts, and converse and reciprocate with those who are interacting with you. Take advantage of Facebook groups to create community, and use Facebook Messenger for interacting with customers. In the words of fast-food chain McDonald's, "Our head of social media is the customer."[7] Yours should be too, fempreneur!

More Social Media Options: TikTok, Snapchat, Pinterest, and YouTube

There are other social media platforms to consider, too. We'll look at TikTok, Snapchat, Pinterest, and YouTube to conclude this Mindset Shift. Depending on your business and customer segments, these options may be right for you and your business.

TikTok

What platform is hotter right now than TikTok? That was a trick question: none! TikTok enables users to create short, looping videos with music and special effects, and it's extremely popular with young adults and teens, with more than 500 million monthly active users. It's also expanding its reach (particularly as a result of the COVID-19 pandemic), with older users flocking to join in on the buzz.[8] Spend an hour watching TikTok videos, and you'll have a strong urge to dance with Derek Hough or follow along with some of the hysterical challenges you see.

Because the platform is newer than many of the others and not without controversy, marketers are still experimenting with ways to best utilize it to reach their target audience. TikTok has its own advertising process and ability to include hyperlinks, and it's often used for increasing brand awareness, particularly among younger target segments. The content on TikTok tends to be lighter and funnier to appeal to the demographic on it. This is the place to try new things and show a different side of your brand personality.

Engagement is the name of the game here, so make the most of challenges, duets, comments, likes, and shares. Challenges are linked to a specific hashtag and work by asking followers to perform the said challenge. Brands often post challenges, as they work well and traditional ads are usually too generic to appeal to this audience. Many brands, including Red Bull and Chipotle, to name a couple, have embraced the app, and the strategies on this platform will only increase as its popularity grows.

Start trying out what might be right for your brand on TikTok, and watch a bunch of videos for inspiration. Use filters and musical overlays, and make sure your content is funny: *funny makes money*. To increase engagement, reply to challenges and use hashtags, while flexing your creative muscles by finding a clever way to showcase your brand. As this app continues to evolve, so will your brand strategies on it. Try new things here—but don't let your teenagers catch you!

Snapchat

Snap is a slightly older social media cousin to TikTok, but it similarly appeals to a younger crowd, with over one million daily active users, most of them between the ages of 18 and 34.[9] Including Snapchat as part of your marketing campaign can be key, depending on your target audience—but no matter what, it's a good platform for building brand awareness. Snap stories are an excellent way to engage brand audiences, and they last for

24 hours. This platform has some cool native features, such as text, emojis, music, filters, geofilters, and more.

Other strategies that brands can use Snapchat for are broadcasting a peek into live events, premiering new products or content, or inviting followers behind the scenes. More brand awareness ideas include offering promotions to those who watch your snap story all the way through and requesting that followers snap a photo with your product or using your service. Finally, Snapchat is also an ideal place for partnering with influencers to appeal to harder-to-reach demographics, so snap to it if this platform makes sense to you, girl.

Pinterest

Pinterest is another platform that may be central to your marketing strategy, depending on your brand. Pinterest is the crafty, creative next-door neighbor of social media—a social network in which users can share and discover new interests through pinning (or posting) and searching through what others have pinned. It's mostly aimed at lifestyle appeal and images.

The number of daily active users on Pinterest is 335 million, with 80 million from the United States. According to Pinterest, 71 percent of users are female and 34 percent are aged 18–29, but the median age on this platform is 40.[10] Top categories on Pinterest include art, art supplies, and hobbies. Another Pinterest stat claims that more than 5 percent of referral traffic to websites comes from Pinterest—that's big news. It is also a serious place to share recipes, so food-related businesses work well here, too.

On Pinterest, users share pins with people similar to them, connecting via things that are of mutual interest. Content on this platform can be scenic, DIY, funny, involve food, or be cute and creative. As a brand, you can grow engagement on Pinterest through pins and likes, and Pinterest can be an attractive platform to market products and grow your customer base by posting powerful images and graphics. Entrepreneurs can increase Pinterest engagement by adding share buttons to their websites and posting personal photos so that customers can put a face to a brand personality.

Consistency and frequency of pins is important for this platform (as with the others). You can create several pins that lead to the same place or use a different pin to help increase views in the Pinterest Smart Feed as well as SEO. Use keywords on your boards, too (boards are where your pins are collected), because they are searchable. It's important to choose a board name with a solid SEO name or something that is searchable, such as "Delicious Cupcakes" or "Modern Interiors," and you can consider creating sections for your boards as well.

Followers are important on Pinterest, but engagement is even more critical. Be certain to confirm your Etsy, YouTube, and Instagram platforms on Pinterest so that you will get people to follow you from them. Your engagement and awareness will increase as well. To further increase engagement, make sure to interact with all of the comments that you get and pin too. Using rich pins helps by displaying pricing information, particularly if you have an ecommerce store; you can also use article or blog pins if you want to drive traffic to your site. You'll be able to apply for rich pins if you have a validated site. On this platform, it's ideal to use vertical images and scale them appropriately.

Stay active and engage with your followers on Pinterest, and track your metrics to further inform your content strategy. According to some Omnicore statistics, "83% of weekly Pinners have made a purchase based on content they saw from brands on Pinterest, and 6 out of 10 millennials use Pinterest to discover new products."[11] So, if Pinterest is a good match for your brand, fempreneur, leverage it to increase purchase activity and awareness for your products!

YouTube

Let's talk about YouTube last, but not least. YouTube, as you well know, is a platform where users upload videos through their YouTube channels. This site is ideal for building your brand presence as well as establishing yourself as a thought leader by creating and publishing video content. Videos often get more engagement on social media platforms, as we've established, and thus are good vehicles to use for growing your brand and connecting with existing and potential customers. You'll want to create a YouTube channel for posting and sharing videos at the very least. YouTube is the second-most-visited website in the world behind Google—people search frequently for all sorts of content on YouTube—so it's an excellent way for your business to be found.[12]

Looking for some tips for video creation and sharing on YouTube? Your videos should have relevant content that is highly searched and informs, educates, or entertains; they must also have high image quality. Ensure that you know exactly who your target audience is before you record any videos to tailor them accordingly.

YouTube is also often thought of as a huge search engine, so if you want to be found (and you do!), you'll have to select your video titles with care. It's important that your videos rank high in the search results. That means you must optimize both your titles and descriptions. To do so, insert a few keywords at the beginning of the title and in the first few sentences of the summary. This way viewers have the best chance of finding your content. There are some tools you can use to identify the best hashtags and keywords for your YouTube videos (like TubeBuddy). If you are selling clothing, for example, it could be that some of the most searched-for phrases are "What to wear to look your best" or "What clothing is age appropriate?" For me, since I work with entrepreneurs, some common phrases are "What are some small business ideas?" and "How to start a business."

In terms of video length, make your actual video around 7–15 minutes (sometimes less), but keep your intro or hook short—no longer than five seconds—or you will lose your viewers' attention. This is where you need to really spark their interest right off the bat. Consider how you personally scroll through and choose YouTube videos. If you have longer watch times associated with your content, the YouTube algorithm will treat it as a video of higher quality. At the end of your videos, you should include information about subscribing to your channel, watching another video, or going to your website or another place to engage with your brand.

It's possible to post all different types of videos on YouTube: they can be educational in nature, they can be in the form of slideshows or reviews, or they can be simply related to or promoting your brand. You might post interviews and videos that entertain as well as live videos—mix it up and see what resonates with your target customers. I've posted a lot of interviews there myself in addition to some course and promotional videos. I love YouTube for its ability to connect me with more followers and as a way to organize and share my video content.

As with the other platforms we've discussed, post frequently. The YouTube algorithm looks favorably on those channels that post more than once a week, which ups your odds of getting recommended in the search results. You should also, at the very least, communicate regularly with your subscribers, showing them that you are dependable and reliable. Loyal subscribers are worth their weight in gold. And you want them to come back for more, don't you? So go out there and get your YouTube channel up and running! Make it your own, LaurenTube, JasmineTube, (Insert Name Here) Tube!

FINAL THOUGHTS

And that wraps up our overview of some of the major social media platforms, from Instagram to Twitter to LinkedIn and more. Getting familiar with and leveraging these social media options is a crucial aspect of Mindset Shift 7. You won't need to be on all of these platforms, but certainly on those where your target audience congregates, and in a way that best builds brand awareness and reach while driving networking and business growth. Have fun with it, too. "If you are on social media, and you are not learning, not laughing, not being inspired or not networking, then you are using it wrong," says Germany Kent, journalist and social media etiquette expert.[13] So, go out there and laugh, inspire, network, and build your base on social media, girl!

LEADING YOUR STARTUP

What's both amazing and terrifying about becoming an entrepreneur is that you are no longer an employee; you are now a leader—leading yourself, your company, and all your employees. This is the chance you've been waiting for after being held back or dealing with bad leaders in the past. As your startup grows, so will your team, and excelling at leadership will be paramount to your success.

In a recent study, Guidant Financial found that one of the main reasons for small business failure is poor recruitment and retention of employees.[1] These employee-related issues are indicative of a lack of entrepreneurial leadership and team-building skills, which may be more challenging for women to hone and develop. This is the result of a gender leadership gap, according to research from the American Association of University Women. This research states simply that "in short, women are much less likely than men to be in leadership positions"—and if women aren't actually serving as leaders in traditional roles at companies where they are employed, then it's difficult to acquire the accompanying leadership skill set when they're ready to launch their own businesses.[2]

This chapter discusses the Mindset Shift required for you to step into your leadership power as the fempreneurial head of your startup. Yes, you can do this, so listen up!

Developing Leadership Skills

Women hold only 26 percent of executive-level positions in S&P 500 companies, according to a University at Buffalo School of Management study, which also found that on average, men are more likely than women to emerge as leaders.[3] Researchers attributed this gender gap to societal pressures that contribute to gender differences in personality traits. Although there are fewer female leaders than male leaders in corporate America, the fact remains that many female leaders are comfortable in the role of managers when working for a traditional employer. Entrepreneurial leadership, however, involves donning a different kind of hat, which can be challenging for many women.

What Is a Leader?

The first part of making this shift is realizing that there is a difference between managers and leaders. Leaders are special and so much more than managers. A manager is simply someone whom people report to on a day-to-day basis, but a leader is an individual whom people look up to and are motivated by: a woman who inspires her team to grow, develop, and perform at higher levels. A leader cares about her employees and their forward trajectory, whereas a manager is interested only in what people can do for him or her personally. Have you ever had to report to someone like that? I have, and it didn't end well: he took credit for all of my work and just kept dumping more on me.

Think of those bad managers in your past and know that their behavior is what you want to avoid. Similarly, reflect back on those leaders who inspired you to reach for more. What was it about them that had that effect on you? I've had several who always pushed or motivated me to grow, and I'm sure that you have, too.

Leading a startup is all about putting others' needs ahead of your own and encouraging progress by setting a positive example, being willing to roll up your sleeves and pitch in, lighting the way for others while inspiring action, and showcasing the talent and accomplishments of your employees. Being a true business leader requires seeing yourself as—and then becoming—someone whom others look up to and are motivated by, and who stirs your team to grow, develop, and perform at higher levels.

Take your leadership role head on and overcome any inhibitions in order to realize your full potential for running a business and heading your startup. Additional support can lift your confidence and business decision making and should be sought after and initiated on your own. It can come in the form of taking leadership courses, reading books and articles, looking for mentors and role models to help you, and developing your emotional intelligence.

Sharpen Your Soft Skills

As part of your leadership development, you must perfect your soft skills, too, including excellent communication, compassion, and the ability to motivate and get along with others. An entrepreneurial leader treats her employees with respect by being open and honest with them. She should communicate with her team frequently, providing candid and constructive feedback so that they can improve on their weaknesses and celebrate and maximize their strengths—showing her team members the way and helping them to grow and find new opportunities while taking a personal interest in them. If you put your staff's needs and desires first, they will never let you down, but "you have to give in order to receive" as Rosie, one of my first managers, told me early on in my career. I always think of her and that quote (thanks, Rosie).

Entrepreneurial leaders must also be able to inspire and bring their team on board with the mission and objectives of their company—and you are no exception, fempreneur! You can motivate others by promoting collaboration, setting clear guidelines, reducing meetings, encouraging autonomy, avoiding micromanagement, and including employees in the development of your startup's strategic objectives. Lead by example and encourage those on your team to relax and just be themselves—you, too, for that matter.

Lead with Both Your Mind and Your Heart

It seems that the more leadership articles I read lately, the more I notice what appears to be a growing distinction between a focus on the numbers and a focus on the people. Do they need to be mutually exclusive, though? The leaders I most admire have a keen ability to swing back and forth between the two. They use their dashboard as a trusted ally but still understand those human factors that impact or can be impacted by the numbers. As a leader, you can't be all heart because there are many swift and difficult decisions to make, but you can't be all metrics either, or you'll lose the connection with those you serve.

I've observed that the highest results tend to come when there is a clear balance between the metrics and the people. I'll admit that I look forward to seeing the weekly stats just as much as the next girl. Strong numbers can be validation for all the time and energy that entire teams have put in—proof that our ideas have merit and potential. But we can't focus solely on the numbers at the exclusion of those we are creating our products and services for, or the teammates who are on the front line bringing those ideas and products to life for our clients. To lose that balance is not good business even if the impact isn't immediate.

Because you are a smart founder, you must place a steady emphasis on both aspects, leading with both mind and heart! And you've got a lot of heart, fempreneur—enough for your business, employees, and all of the other important people in your life! Getting this equilibrium down will be central to this phase of your Mindset Shift and leadership growth.

Know Your Ins and Outs

Great female leaders are able to navigate and communicate well, both within and outside their organization—with everyone from subordinates and partners to competitors and clients. The ability to interact and encourage as a leader will propel your startup forward. You also need to be willing to delegate and provide guidance for those you hire: they can't read your mind (well, not unless you've launched a psychic startup), so become skilled at communicating your expectations and setting the bar for success.

Employ Savvy Staffing

Leadership also has to do with staffing and retention of your employees. When adding to your team, look for employees who are hardworking, personable, and willing to learn, as you want to foster the ability for your employees to grow with your company and juggle varying responsibilities. Until you're able to hire a larger staff, you'll all be wearing numerous hats—some fancy (Kentucky Derby fedoras) and some the straw kind you wear while gardening outside—so you will need someone who can adapt to those many styles.

Focus on retention, too: encourage your team to stay by rewarding their efforts and letting them know that they are appreciated. It's expensive to find, hire, and train new employees, and you want to maintain and grow the talent that you already have in place, in line with this Mindset Shift.

Use Your Intuition

Over the years, I've also learned to rely heavily on my intuition, and women leaders are lucky in this regard, having sharpened our female intuition over time. If you sense there is a problem or something going on with an employee, chances are you're right. I once had a woman on my team who started skipping our meetings and wasn't joining in on our group chats, so I gave her a call. It turns out that she was having some health issues that had nothing to do with work. You just never know what is happening with people sometimes, so follow your gut and intervene.

Similarly, if something doesn't feel right about someone you are thinking about hiring, then don't hire that person. Trust your Spidey-senses. If you perceive that your team is feeling down—perhaps you are pushing them too hard or they don't feel appreciated—do what you can to pick them up and back off, if that's what's needed. Your intuition will show you the way, and as a leader, I've relied heavily on it in numerous roles (it's never let me down). You should lean on it, too, when leading your startup team.

Look to Role Models and Personality Tests

If you're struggling to enhance your leadership traits, look for positive examples in some female leaders you admire. Analyze their performance and presence, and ascertain what it is that you like about them by watching their speeches and trying to emulate the way they communicate. They don't have to be celebrities or anyone famous; they should just be women who inspire you. Research them, see what they do, and then try to mimic them, but in your own way.

We all need role models to look up to, so if there aren't any in your life, go out there and find them. Connect with them online, read their books, and watch their videos. You can learn a lot by watching others or seeking out a mentor (as mentioned previously)—paid or otherwise—who can help you up your leadership game. It's definitely a good idea to get someone else behind you and your goals during this Mindset Shift.

It can be worthwhile to take an online personality test to determine what your personality type is, including whether you are introverted or extroverted, observant or intuitive, thinking vs. feeling, judging vs. prospecting, or assertive vs. turbulent. Personality test results can help you identify your strengths and weaknesses and understand how they impact your workplace performance and leadership style.

For example, 16Personalities.com is a site I've used before with one such test. This test identified me as a "Campaigner Personality" type (ENFP—Extroverted, Intuitive, Feeling, Perceptive). Here's the summary of that personality type:

> The Campaigner personality is a true free spirit. They are often the life of the party, but unlike types in the Explorer Role group, Campaigners are less interested in the sheer excitement and pleasure of the moment than they are in enjoying the social and emotional connections they make with others. Charming, independent, energetic and compassionate, the 7% of the population that they comprise can certainly be felt in any crowd.[4]

What's amusing is that your test results also provide examples of characters from TV shows and movies that share your personality type. For instance, two famous Campaigners are Michael Scott from *The Office* and Carrie Bradshaw from *Sex and the City*. Although they have their quirks, they are certainly both ones to get behind a cause or idea, and I am, too!

As outlandish as it may seem, I recognize their campaigning styles in my own leadership, where I am often trying to push new initiatives and rally my team.

To get a better understanding of what the analysis for each personality type is like, here's another snippet from my results:

> As managers, Campaigner personalities behave much like they do as colleagues—they establish real friendships and use their broad popularity to inspire and motivate, taking on the role of leader, working alongside their subordinates, rather than shouting from behind their desks. Campaigners will tend to believe in the concept of intrinsic motivation, the idea that things are worth doing for their own sake, not because of some convoluted system of punishments and rewards. Unfortunately, not everyone buys into this philosophy—challenges arise when faced with subordinates who actually prefer to be closely directed, with clearly defined objectives and timetables, people who are just doing their job.

These results ring true when I reflect upon my personal leadership style. Interesting, isn't it? What's cool about these types of tests is that they can shed light on your strengths and weaknesses and how you can enhance leadership at your startup and when interacting with colleagues and others. You need to know yourself in order to improve your ability to deal with and inspire your team, so take a personality test and see what insight you can glean. I, for one, have incorporated what I've learned into my leadership toolbox. Encourage your employees to do so as well, as it will enable you to better understand and motivate them, too.

Become a Role Model

In general, and no matter what your personality type, being an excellent leader involves being a good role model. Act as if someone is always witnessing your behavior even when they are not, be consistent and fair, and treat people the way you'd want to be treated. Avoid playing favorites (even if you have them), and make sure that everyone feels valued; otherwise, they won't be there long. Do what you can to become more likeable as well by showing respect, listening, being polite, smiling more, and making eye contact while you pay attention to what people say, showing a genuine interest in them.

As a business leader, you should be extremely people-oriented and focused. You must also be very strategic, make hard decisions, and lead by example. Be sure to dress the part as well, so that people will look up to and be inspired by you (choosing your new look will be fun, too), and endeavor to be enthusiastic and positive, no matter what the circumstances.

Startup leaders should be decisive, candid, and organized, and they should follow through with what they say they are going to do. There is nothing worse than promising something to one of your team members and then not delivering on it—you'll lose them. Mastering the skills and traits I've mentioned are central to this Mindset Shift, and you can do it, girl. I have faith in you.

Being Flexible with Your Team

Another part of this entrepreneurial leadership Mindset Shift involves understanding your employees' needs and priorities. One critical area—particularly in the new post-COVID-19 world—relates to the importance of offering employees flexibility in the workplace. Today, this is necessary not only so employees can maintain proper work-life integration, but for safety reasons as well. Once you become a woman business owner, you must adopt a mindset of flexibility to work with the multiple demands of your staff, instead of competing against these personal responsibilities, and creatively meet current and potential employees' demands by incorporating flexible schedules to foster greater employee satisfaction.

Show You Care and Offset Pressure

There's so much pressure being placed on people now, and we are all juggling both at work and in our personal lives. If you give your team members some flexibility in order to meet all of their responsibilities, you are letting them know that you care about them and their well-being. When people see that you care, they'll care more, too: again, you get what you give. The more in balance your employees are, the happier and more productive they will be on the job, which will lead to fewer mistakes, enhanced communication, higher satisfaction, and an overall positive working environment for both coworkers and clients.

Additionally, if you offer flexible scheduling, you'll attract candidates who might not otherwise be available—a perk that can potentially be more alluring than a higher salary. It comes back to the old debate about what is more important, money or time? If time is more important, there will be a certain set of applicants that will be more interested in flexibility and probably more loyal to a company that embraces it. By allowing for that flexibility, you are signaling that you are there for them and understand that they have other obligations outside of the workplace to consider. Also, by working with their multiple demands instead of combating them, you are embracing the employee as a complete person and offering an understanding and supportive environment.

For example, as a single mother, I worked for one company at a lower salary for years because they allowed me to work remotely, which was more conducive to my busy and stretched lifestyle. As I mentioned previously, this flexibility is particularly important during recent times like dealing with COVID-19 and the additional stressors that it placed on all employees, including childcare, homeschooling, and elder-care responsibilities.

Consider Unlimited PTO

Unlimited paid time off (PTO) can also be a very attractive perk for job candidates who want to maintain equilibrium and who have other goals or obligations. With the proper parameters in place, unlimited PTO programs will lure applicants who are looking for a different, more balanced set of benefits or perks.

In today's competitive work environment, entrepreneurial leaders must get creative to meet potential employees' demands and to attract the best possible candidates. By incorporating and accommodating flexible schedules, female business owners will engage with more potential candidates and foster greater contentment and overall satisfaction with their employees. You'll also flex and build your leadership muscles in the process, further completing this Mindset Shift to lead your startup to success.

Managing Remote Teams

Whereas the traditional world of work relied on a mindset of managing and leading in-house staff, today's women entrepreneurs—again, especially in light of recent changes—will likely be managing remote teams. This new reality requires a subsequent Mindset Shift away from the idea that employees can only be effectively managed in person to instead embracing the idea of a more flexible work arrangement in which team members may be working different hours than their manager.

Emphasize Accomplishments, Not Hours

In line with this Mindset Shift, you will need to learn how to focus on an employee's individual productivity and ability to meet predefined milestones and goals, rather than counting hours or times of day on the job. Other strategies include communicating candidly about expectations in advance regarding schedules, productivity, deadlines, virtual meeting times, and follow-up; building trust in remote employees; and providing support to remote workers. Let's get to it and delve into these strategies because this will be an important part of your leadership role.

When it comes to managing people who work from home, as I do, you have to embrace the idea of flex schedules. Many employees prefer to work remotely in order to accommodate their other obligations and interests. Don't be alarmed if your team members are not working the same hours as you—perhaps they are getting more done in the evenings or on the weekends. Focus instead on their individual accomplishments and whether or not they are meeting their milestones and goals, as this will ease your anxiety while ensuring that you're getting results.

Communicate

Have a candid and authentic discussion and put expectations in place when it comes to your employees' schedule and productivity. Which deadlines are negotiable, and which are more rigid and fixed? How frequently will you touch base? The goal here is also balance, not too much and not too little. Don't be a micromanager, but don't be too checked out either.

Trust that remote employees are performing at optimal levels, but provide guardrails to ensure that it is actually happening while remaining supportive and aware. If performance changes need to be made, communicate future expectations and follow up. The same applies to relationships with contractors where you must also put the proper parameters in place. Nothing goes smoothly if we don't talk about it, so get comfortable speaking up, girl.

If you're dealing with an employee who is having a hard time embracing remote working arrangements, get to the heart of the resistance and find a way to provide support or additional information to bring him or her on board with the concept. Our business environment continues to change and evolve, so working from home will grow to become even more of the norm and will also remain a powerful incentive for a certain pool of talent. Startups are ideal for these types of remote working relationships, so take advantage and adapt accordingly as an up-and-coming leader.

Expressing Gratitude to Employees

As another facet of this Mindset Shift, you should also infuse gratitude into your leadership plan. Gratitude enhances the employee experience in many ways. We are so often caught up in the negative, or the mundane, that we fail to see all the positive things happening around us and to truly appreciate the amazing people and opportunities that we have in our lives, especially at work.

When there is a lack of gratitude, morale is negatively affected. Conversely, when employees feel that we are grateful for and truly appreciate them, they come to know that they are valued and that their work has meaning, and they also become more grateful in return. It's a circular process, and an attitude of gratitude spreads from the top down, all the way to clients. As an entrepreneur, you're at the top and will set the vibe for your tribe.

Gratitude can benefit women business owners immensely, and keeping a gratitude journal is a good way to begin. In it, state one to three things, related to your startup and those you manage, that you are grateful for, and ask team members to do the same. Do this every day. You can even take it a step further and share your journals, perhaps during a meeting or at a team event. This journaling process will start to shift your mindset, and that of your staff, and you will begin to become more aware of all that you have to be appreciative of. It will ultimately bring the team closer together, too, because you will begin to truly see each other and the value that each member brings to the group. Try it. I do this, and I love writing down all of the good stuff and then going back and looking it over. It makes me smile every time.

Fostering Thankfulness

There are several other ways that fempreneurs can build this sort of culture at their startup, and it begins with implementing activities that foster thankfulness. Many organizations have meetings and events where they bring employees together; recently, these have been done more virtually. Focus those events on team-building activities (instead of presentations or lectures) that boost morale and build a positive environment. Rather than giving out individual awards, present a small award to each member of the team and tell every person why you are grateful for him or her and what value he or she brings to the business. This activity lifts the team as a whole and gets everyone to focus on the positive in each member, which enhances overall gratitude. I did this once with individually inscribed medals, but any little trinket will work.

It's also fun to try a roundtable activity where you ask everyone to draw a picture of their personal journey at the company, highlighting what they've been appreciative of or excited about along the way. When everyone's finished, go around the table (or take turns on a virtual call) and ask them, individually, to showcase their drawings and discuss their path and its highlights. This is storytelling at its best, with a lens of gratitude. You'll be amazed at what you can learn about everyone and how much the team will enjoy it, too, while focusing on all that they have to be thankful for at work. Don't forget to take pictures and post them so that other stakeholders can see and share them as well.

I facilitated this activity at a team event one year with tremendous results. All of the employees enjoyed learning more about each other and their individual journeys. We even told the stories while eating s'mores around a pretend campfire, and we also had a lot of fun simulating day-to-day activities that our customers face and respond to. We wrote them down on golf balls and then tried to get them from one side of the room to another. These sorts of team builders do wonders for employee bonding, so incorporate them at your startup when you can.

There are many business benefits associated with cultivating an attitude of gratitude at your company, including a boost in employee morale and satisfaction, higher retention, and an increase in the level of customer service to both internal and external customers. When employees are truly happy and thankful, your clients will be, too, and that will positively impact your bottom line—which you will be grateful for as well.

Pay It Forward, Give It Backward

As a business leader, you must also pay it forward and give it backward. What I mean is that you have to be thankful for those who have helped you along the path of your entrepreneurial journey. No one becomes successful on their own; there are doors and windows opened for each of us. Don't take that help and those opportunities for granted. Maintain your connections and personal relationships and be appreciative of the assistance you've received. Embrace gratitude, and also be sure to pass opportunities along to those who are coming up after you. The world is a circle, and true fempreneurs lift up and help each other. So, the next time someone knocks on your door or window, support them when you can. Along my journey, people have helped me from stepping-stone to stepping-stone, and I've tried to turn back and help others move from stone to stone as well. This generosity of spirit is a key part of your Mindset Shift as a fempreneurial leader.

Give back, too, if possible. There are so many ways that you can contribute to worthy causes. Have your startup sponsor a charity event or luncheon, or provide excess products or a small portion of your bottom line to a nonprofit. Social awareness and success are often intertwined, so do what you can to contribute, even if it's just sharing your expertise. As we've talked about previously, people are more willing to purchase from companies that support charities and/or social causes. You can pick a nonprofit that aligns with your organization or industry or support another that is near and dear to your heart. I volunteer regularly for several nonprofits here in Charlotte, North Carolina. The point is to just make a difference, and helping others is yet another facet of this Mindset Shift.

Set the Example

In general, as the head of your startup, you're setting the example, from giving back to giving it your all, so be strong and learn to embrace failure and setbacks when you first start out; these hindrances are inevitable. It's very challenging and sometimes overwhelming to be a new business owner. Therefore, you must find that inner resolve to keep moving forward while you're getting your company off the ground. Your employees will react to disappointment and hindrances the way you do, so own and welcome them. Failure is good in business: it means that you are innovating and pushing ahead.

For entrepreneurs, it's also critical to commit to the process and remain passionate and driven as your company grows so you can stay in it for the long haul that it will take to get your business thriving. As the founder, you pass your passion along to the rest of the startup team. Your enthusiasm will ignite your employees to achieve great things and take your organization to new heights while providing the utmost level of service for your clients. As singer and actress Dolly Parton said, "If your actions create a legacy that inspires others to dream more, learn more, do more and become more, then you are an excellent leader."[5] Smart words coming from a lady who knows the value of entrepreneurship and the lack of fulfillment associated with a corporate gig, as she sang about in her famous song "9 to 5." How many of you are out there barely getting by, with all taking and no giving? Holler!

Leading with Empathy

Another key component of a leadership Mindset Shift for women entrepreneurs involves the ability to understand what others need and want. To do this you must tap into empathic leadership, servant leadership, open-mindedness, and relationship building.

Empathy has served me well over the years. The ability to relate to others is critical and will never let you down. Empathy enables you to lead teams, earn respect and friends, and understand what people are going through in order to react appropriately. When you look at people as individuals with unique needs, you are getting to know what motivates them and makes them tick. You are also figuring out what they'll respond to while bonding with them on a deeper level. Our ability to empathize prevents us from overreacting or behaving in a self-centered manner, thus allowing us to become better communicators who work toward a common good and forge mutually beneficial relationships.

Professionally, it involves servant leadership and treating others how we'd like to be treated. Personally, it involves open-mindedness and giving back. Empathy is a critical life skill and will help you build relationships both on and off the job. This quality has helped me often in my life, both when leading entrepreneurial teams and developing friendships. As Maya Angelou said, "I've learned that people will forget what you said, people will forget what you did, but people will never forget how you made them feel."[6] Make your team feel good, fempreneur!

Be a Servant Leader

Servant leadership encompasses giving without receiving—in other words, leading in an attempt to serve the people around you. This is a leadership imperative, and you do it by figuring out ways to support and keep your employees and by seeking frequent feedback as well. Servant leadership puts people above processes, and this emphasis has a positive impact on the work environment, customers, and the business as a whole.

In order to practice what you preach, you should focus on your employees' needs—striving to meet them—not catering to their feelings, which is different. This practice consists of listening, compassion, building community, and awareness. It also encompasses your ability to see the big picture and persuade others to strive for your startup's big dreams and goals.

To be a servant leader, you first have to become very self-aware. Self-awareness is the ability to step outside oneself and analyze your behavior and how it impacts and affects others. Self-awareness also includes assessing your strengths and weaknesses, so you can work to maximize your skills and lessen and improve your areas of deficit.

Lastly, as an empathetic leader, you'll also be acting as a mentor to your employees, ensuring that they are supported and have the resources and tools to achieve their goals. As part of that, you must create a work environment that enables them to be happy and engaged and a workplace that is healthy. Work to develop rapport and an authentic connection with them—be warm and personable in your interactions, highlight their abilities, and help them overcome their challenges.

Further, be sure to give your employees stretch goals and glamorous projects that enable them to shine. Focus that spotlight directly on their path, and they will climb to new heights. I once led an employee who was at first uncertain, but I took her under my wing, gave her lots of encouragement and guidance, and she has gone on to achieve some major triumphs. With the right nurturing, your employees will too.

FINAL THOUGHTS

A Mindset Shift is the key to growing these solid interpersonal relationships because nothing valuable happens automatically. You have to work at any relationship to make it strong. Your hustle is about employee and client rapport, not sales. Make the grit and persistence we've talked about a part of your startup culture when serving stakeholders, and ensure that everyone at your company is attending to clients and building bridges, while being a worthy role model and living it.

If you want your team to be persistent and gritty, infuse persistence and grittiness into your culture. This is what will set the foundation for your organization. In shaping your startup's vibe, demonstrate a commitment to your goals and then help your team develop the grit necessary to achieve them, to keep your company moving forward as you master and hone this critical Mindset Shift.

Let's close this chapter with the words of singer and songwriter Beyoncé, "We need to reshape our own perception of how we view ourselves. We have to step up as women and take the lead."[7] Girl, charge forth and take the lead at your business and in your life!

GOING INTO GROWTH MODE

You're gaining traction as a startup maven—glowing and now ready to start growing. This chapter shows you how to embrace the Mindset Shift necessary to persist and keep reinventing your business as needed. We'll get into how you can develop a growth-mode mentality in terms of three key areas—resilience, reinvention/rebranding, and innovation/creativity—to catapult your venture to long-term success. I know you're ready now, so let's go!

Developing Resilience

As a fempreneur, you'll need to cultivate a mindset of resilience to help you bounce back from the inevitable obstacles associated with launching and running a startup. Some days, you are going to feel like you're being bounced around on the heavy-duty setting in your washing machine, so you'll need the strength to climb into the dryer and get those wrinkles out! I've been there before: losing a large client, hitting a major snag with products, or having to deal with some other type of complicated issue. You'll face similar situations, too. We'll discuss how you can develop mental strength, overcome adversity, adapt to change, pivot after failure, deal with setbacks, increase confidence in your power, and learn to reframe difficult situations—nothing is insurmountable.

You are a business owner now. You will not win every fight you're in, and you'll lose supporters and backers along the way. If the path to entrepreneurship were an easy one, there would be many more successful entrepreneurs out there. In order to grow and thrive in business, you need to develop the ability to overcome hindrances and keep trudging along as you face failures, setbacks, and disappointments. These pitfalls will be interwoven with opportunities and successes, and you must be resourceful as a leader in order to bounce back, keep moving forward, and grab those lucrative, new opportunities as they arise.

Resilience is something that I have developed and mastered out of necessity. When my two daughters were only two and four years old, my husband passed away unexpectedly in a helicopter accident. I was working two jobs at the time and midway through getting my PhD. I thought I would never make it through—that I'd never be able to work, take care of my children, and complete my doctorate. But you know what? I did. I raised my two girls on my own, finished that PhD, and blossomed both personally and professionally. I also went on to launch a brand and write two books. If I didn't pull on my resilience during those tough times, that would have never happened.

You can do this, too, because inevitably, we'll all experience snags as entrepreneurs, and resilience helps us keep progressing and enables us to deal with problems. Resilient women are mentally tough, able to overcome adversity, and know how to cope and adapt without getting stuck. Being quick to recover is vital for when we hit those challenges. We will sometimes lose (deals or support) and must pivot in order to keep moving ahead. Leading a startup is about reinvention and growth.

Failure makes us stronger, so it's essential to own it and take with us the lessons we learned: we've got to adjust, adapt, and move our companies along. There are many times when I didn't get opportunities that I was so sure I would get. In those cases, I had no choice but to try something else and find another way. You should, too, and, as part of that, don't spin your wheels chasing after something that is not meant to be. There is something else better that is just around the corner, and it's got your name on it in ALL CAPS!

Everyone has resilience but at differing levels. Your success has to do with how you put it to use and how you deal with problems and setbacks as a rule, but the good news is that your resilience level is not fixed. There are ways that you can increase it.

The first thing you can do is to believe in yourself and have more confidence in your abilities and strengths. We've talked about this before: you are amazing, so keep telling yourself that! Hell, shout it from the rooftops if you need to! You can also focus on becoming more positive. When you hit a difficulty, don't drown in the misery. Instead, come up with a plan. How are you going to tackle this roadblock and regroup without giving in to feelings of defeat? Lay out your next steps and then execute them because you are now a master time manipulator and planning diva. You have many talents.

Improve Your Communication and Problem-Solving Capabilities

Work on your communication skills, too. If you have an issue with a colleague or client, ask questions and get feedback. If you get a dismissal from a sales prospect, don't let that decision maker escape without telling you the reason they decided not to hire you. Further, try to talk them out of their decision if you can and turn it around. There have been times when something happened that didn't seem fair or clear to me until I asked for and got clarification. It's difficult to guess what happened; ask the one who made the decision instead.

For example, once I didn't understand why I wasn't considered for a professional opportunity. Another time, a client was upset about something that wasn't clear-cut. I could have merely guessed why this happened, but instead I dug deeper and got feedback from both of the parties involved. And guess what? The reasons they gave were not what I'd imagined on my own. On another occasion, a pitch of mine was rejected, but when I asked for more information, I was able to turn it around and get the deal. Once you have the answers, you can adjust and make changes moving forward. I've done this many times. I've flipped situations to my favor and broken relationships toward repair.

Honing your problem-solving skills will also be crucial. Visualize and clarify outcomes and then make plans and track your progress. When thinking about an issue, focus on the solution instead of the problem.

The problem is the negative; the solution is the positive. This can be challenging, I know, because our instinct is to dwell on the problem. But as a fempreneur, you fix things. The solution is your BFF, and the problem your frenemy—remember that.

It can also be helpful to ask yourself *why* questions. Why is this happening? Why did this break? Why was another company chosen? Why don't I live next door to Bradley Cooper (JK)? Simplify the issue, and don't overly complicate the solution.

Lastly, brainstorm as many possible fixes to your problem as you can before choosing one. The easiest fix is typically not the best, so resist the urge to cheat by grabbing a quick solution. Pretend this is a test and your mentor is watching you like a hawk! Be accountable to the best, because you are at that level now!

Become More Patient and Positive

In order to develop your resilience, you must simultaneously develop your patience. I will tell you that patience has always been (and still often is) a challenge for me, but it's something that I continue to work on. Don't get discouraged; things will happen for you when the timing is right, and your moment is approaching.

Practice developing your patience by making yourself wait on things, such as eating, buying, or taking action. Realize what makes you anxious, and work to overcome it. Avoid instant gratification. For example, when you consider getting a second helping of dinner or buying something that you don't really need, wait. Pause on that piece of cake or before making a knee-jerk action. Also, try to wait before speaking: train yourself to think first—another toughie. Learn to recognize triggers and employ positive self-talk to get you through when your impatience starts kicking in. Attempt to be patient for an entire day and build on that.

Teach yourself to see the bright side, too, because with every negative, there is always a positive. Where is it? Perhaps you got the feedback you needed to take your product or service to the next level. Or you realized where your weakness was compared to your competitors. All of your failures are leading you to something else, something better. Think of your journey as a path; you simply need to follow a few zigzags to get there. There are no straight lines in entrepreneurship, so zig, baby, zig!

Focus and Energize

To successfully bounce back, you need to eliminate distractions. We talked earlier about the ways you can reduce them (Mindset Shift 4), so you are well versed. Consider what can deter you and whether or not you have the time and energy to get to where you want to be.

Sometimes you'll have to get reenergized and do the things that give you that additional boost and momentum. Maybe it's playing music or having dinner with friends. I always feel so much better after I find time for a good, solid workout. Maybe it's running or dancing for you. Always accept yourself (good and bad) and believe that you can overcome anything, because you know what? You can. I believe in you, fempreneur.

Accept Change

Resilient fempreneurs like you welcome change. Don't panic when there is a kink in the plan; instead, simply make new preparations toward your goal, adjust, and find perspective. It's usually not the end of the road and only a minor hindrance. We live in a world of constant disruption, and as a business owner, you'll need to get extremely comfortable with that. If you don't pivot, you won't be able to compete.

You can always learn from your past, too, so make reflection your new best friend. How have you been able to overcome similar obstacles before? What got you through? Perhaps you can go to others for strength: persuade them to give you reminders and clues if you need them. I always call my mom for this sort of advice (don't judge me).

Get Unstuck

If you're really stuck, you can get help. Join groups and feed off the energy of other people moving ahead toward the same goals. Read books on resilience and achievement. Consider finding a coach. Sometimes, one single session is all you need to recharge your battery. It can get lonely as an entrepreneur. So many female business owners have come to me for this very reason, and I've loved talking them through their next moves. I've also sought help before when I was feeling stalled or off-kilter. It's a magnificent way to put extra energy behind your venture or idea. If you are experiencing severe self-doubt or negative thoughts, you can always pull in a counselor to help you sort through your feelings.

Charge On

At the end of the day, you need to keep charging ahead, and this begins with laying out your plans and next steps. It's what separates those who succeed from those who fail. In the face of setbacks, you have to pick yourself up, dust yourself off, straighten your skirt, and rise to the challenge.

Regroup and reformulate your goals. Ask yourself some tough questions:

- What do you really want to achieve?
- What can you improve on and when?
- Are you really committed to making it happen?
- What can stop you?
- What part of this do you find most overwhelming, and why?
- Are you experiencing any negative self-talk?
- What are your biggest sources of stress, and what can you do to keep them at bay?

Keep it positive, of course. Although you might love to throw yourself a pity party or smash a dish in protest, does it really make sense now that you're a successful entrepreneur? Not so much.

Imagine Something Better

When you encounter a setback or failure, train yourself to dream up new possibilities. Maybe there is a bigger deal on the horizon, or perhaps that client is not as good as the 10 new ones that you'll get next month and who will take less of your time. Determine what can now come about as a consequence of this shift. Has it opened you up to conquer something else? What is newly possible, and how can you get there? Make a list, because putting it on paper brings you one step closer to making it a reality—it's a written contract with yourself. You deserve that deal, so sign it, stamp it, and move on it.

Reframe Your View

Being resilient hinges on your ability to reframe and adjust, so uncover any fears and hidden risks that may thwart your progress. You can't control what happens to you, but you can control how you react to it. Reframing begins with recognizing negative thoughts and turning them into positive thoughts. It's okay to be disappointed, but don't live there. Find a way to put an optimistic spin on whatever happens. There is no specific meaning to any event or experience. We are the ones who assign it a meaning. It's that simple.

One way to launch this reframing process is to start recognizing your thoughts by writing them down in a thought journal. As soon as a situation happens, chronicle your negative thinking related to it, recognizing and reframing your perception. It can also help to wear a band around your wrist. Every time you have a negative inkling, give the band a snap. Ouch! It seems silly, but it can really stop your pessimism right away through conditioning.

Regroup and brainstorm. What are some possible fixes to your jam? Do you have a contingency plan? If not, you should start making that a part of your best practices moving forward. In the words of award-winning entrepreneur and founder of Li-Da Foods Rita Zahara, "When your world is in pieces, you can choose to see it as crumbling or building. Your attitude, resilience, and determination mark the difference."[1] Be a builder, not a crumbling sugar cookie, fempreneur.

Develop Coping Strategies

You should also develop coping strategies for regrouping—that is, learning to release your emotions and not keeping them bottled up inside. Feel them, but don't wallow in them. If you are experiencing distress, learn to distract yourself with activities and people you enjoy. Plan an outing, get some fresh air, reward yourself. I like boxing as a release—hitting a bag, not a person (duh). You should find your own release. Process and get rid of any anger that you are feeling, as it won't serve you well over the long run. Acquire ways to relax and reset your mindset, and then visualize your next move. What is it? When will you start? What will it take to make it happen?

Come Up with an Alternative Plan

As I mentioned in Mindset Shift 2, make it part of every day to develop a plan B, and have a C, D, and E, too, just in case. If you've reached the end of the alphabet, use Plan A-2 or start using emojis. As the old saying goes, "If at first you don't succeed, try, try again." Always embrace a challenge, because if you are pushing yourself hard, you are growing a lot more. Find the fun in it, rise to the occasion, and adopt a can-do attitude to make things happen.

I love a good challenge, particularly when someone thinks I can't do something. It's sort of like a duel that makes me say, "Oh, yeah, I'll show you." I guess I should say thanks for the nudge. You should too, girl. Show 'em what you got!

Remind Yourself to Be Resilient

It can be useful to give yourself resiliency prompts and reminders. Find a beloved inspirational quote and display it at your startup where you can readily see it when you need a little boost. One of my favorites is Henry David Thoreau's "In the long run, we only hit what we aim at."[2] I have it hanging on my fridge to remind me to always endeavor to aim big. You can get whatever you really try for, so click your heels three times and focus.

Hold yourself accountable by setting calendar check-ins regarding your new goals. Identify someone you can either celebrate with or lean on if things don't go the way that you'd hoped initially. The point is, plan a celebration either way because even failures are worth embracing. You tried and you put yourself out there. You stretched, but it just didn't work out this time. It will eventually. Come up with something that helps you deal— your go-to *deal-with-it* strategy and method to reflect and recharge. Mine has always been getting outdoors. As Helen Keller, the resilient female icon, said, "We could never learn to be brave and patient if there were only joy in the world."[3] You said it, Helen.

Reinventing and Rebranding Your Business

While leading your startup, you'll need to constantly reinvent and rebrand your business: entrepreneurship isn't an occupation where you can sit back and rest on your laurels. Embracing this is another critical facet of your Mindset Shift. When you launch a company, you need to adopt an attitude that helps you take market shifts and other changes in stride, which requires being comfortable with disruption and evolving. We'll get into a number of strategies to do so, such as continuous learning to stay ahead of the curve in your industry; pacing yourself by making small, step-by-step improvements; and rebooting and rebranding in response to evolving market conditions. This section will further unleash the disruptor in you: she is in there and ready to take action!

Running a business is a never-ending process. Just when you think you've got everything about right, or the way you want it, it's time to change and readjust as the market shifts. Keep learning new skills and stay abreast of movements in your industry. When adjusting, do things a little at a time, avoiding the urge to do everything at once. Progress involves incremental improvement and change, so stop every now and again and assess how far you've come on your entrepreneurial journey. You may be shocked at the amount of headway you've made, even when it often feels that you are sitting still. It might be that you are only moving forward slowly, but it's still progress.

Keep a journal that chronicles your achievements, and refer back to it and use it to formulate new goals after you've hit your initial milestones. Make it fun, too, by thinking of it as your brag book or the eventual story of how you hit it big—the early years are what make that possible. Who knows, maybe they'll turn it into a screenplay one day. Wow! Who would you choose to play you?

Make time to take inventory and focus on your accomplishments. What have you done well, and what do you need to improve? Always keep your most intense concentration on the good. Declutter from time to time by getting rid of anything that no longer serves you or your business (both physically and mentally), and reorganize and revisit often.

As the leader of your brand and band, you'll also need to reboot occasionally as market conditions morph and evolve. Entrepreneurship encompasses steady innovation and building on your initial growth and success. Rebranding is especially critical when sales or traffic is down. Do your due diligence before embarking on this endeavor through exhaustive market research, with your current customers being central to the process and equation, and plan every detail related to your rebranding before rolling it out.

When your target market has shifted, when there has been an increase in new competitors, or if changes in technology or new trends have taken hold in your industry, rebranding is also needed. In addition, it can be important if you never really had a solid brand strategy in the first place, or if your brand has become stale or dated. Sometimes a light tweak is all that's necessary, and other times your brand will need a complete overhaul. Analyze your current strategies and processes, and then ascertain what you should keep and what you would like to do away with. Whatever is still working well, retain—there's no need to reinvent the wheel here. Pay attention to what your competition is doing, and bring employees and other stakeholders into the discussion as well. Together, you'll come up with a better and more applicable rebranding strategy.

Once your plan is in place, launch and then promote, promote, promote. You want the world to know how you've changed, improved, and will now better serve your customers' needs. Never be complacent. You are a mover, shaker, and pioneer at heart. Push, push, and then push some more.

Being Innovative

Part of the reinvention and rebranding process involves adopting a mindset of constant innovation and creativity at your startup. Ensure that you are continually pushing the envelope by coming up with new ways of doing things and thinking. These can be changes to something within your business or something that adds to your industry. This section covers the mental shifts that are required to do so, whether you're transforming a process or a product.

Many people define innovation as breaking through boundaries to add value for your customers, which encompasses coming up with new ideas, fresh thinking, and brainstorming. There is a difference between innovation and improvement, however. All innovations are improvements (because they involve a new idea), but not all improvements are innovations (because they are often merely upgrades to existing ideas).

Innovative people have certain characteristics: they are your rebels (think leather jackets and laptops), who push limits and don't like to follow rules; they tend to be super-charged, creative go-getters who make things happen, and they are also very curious and quick to spot problems. Innovators are extremely independent and really into what they do, typically have a good sense of humor, and can laugh at themselves. (I know I can. I do a lot of silly stuff.) They also want to take action and have the next big breakthrough—ambition drives them. (Did someone say "type A"? Hear, hear.) I'm sure that you have many of these traits already and should now kick them into overdrive.

Don't continue to do things the same way just because they've always been done that way. Instead, you must look for new approaches, and as a great leader, you shouldn't shy away from risks. Innovators want to do it quickly, so they often take shortcuts to get there faster, not getting mired down in processes. And these women aren't having self-esteem issues either; they are very confident and open. Disruptors are flexible when things go wrong, network with others to get ideas, value people and teams, and know how to inspire everyone to work together to make big breakthroughs. Learn to adopt these same best practices.

Our country has never had a shortage of innovative women, ranging from Jeanne Villepreux-Power, the creator of the aquarium, and Josephine Cochrane, who invented the dishwasher—God bless her!—to modern disruptors like Oprah Winfrey and Sara Blakely. If you feel that you aren't particularly disruptive or innovative, that's okay. There are things that you can do to build these qualities, starting with transforming the way you think. You must first take control of fear, learn to embrace risks, and power through scary situations. It's not that innovative people don't experience fear; they just don't let it rule their decisions, and they learn to ignore it (like that annoying coworker, remember him?). There are many other methods to boost innovation too. Let's look at some of my favorites.

Phone a Friend

If you feel that you've hit a wall innovatively speaking, dial up a friend. You can become more inventive by asking other people for their thoughts on what you're doing or working on. I'm sure that you are already doing this when you hit other stumbling blocks or barriers in your life—turning to your "ride or dies," or those people you can go to for help, no matter what. Now, you need to find your innovation "ride or dies."

Become More Curious

Try to cultivate your curiosity if it doesn't come naturally for you. Start by asking questions and strive to become a person who takes action when they spot something out of the norm or an opportunity to improve something. Begin to ponder the mysteries in the world that surrounds you, particularly through the lens of how it can make you grow as a savvy businesswoman.

Embrace the Extreme

Innovative women learn to embrace that extreme, excessive side of themselves, latching on to those outrageous ideas and running with them. They think really big to start and only bring it down in relation to their ability to execute, so get into that habit. Another way to push boundaries is to not settle for the first solution. Always keep searching, and learn to ignore your expertise, which can sometimes inhibit you, disruptively speaking.

It also pays to dismiss obvious solutions or existing ideas. If you're lacking inspiration, look to breakthroughs from pioneering companies. Although their solutions may not relate directly to your business, they might inspire you to come up with one of your own. So browse around. In other words, stalk other startups for innovation hacks that you can try!

Look to the Unrelated

To become more of a disruptor, it can also help to turn toward those things that are unrelated. There are so many ways that you can do this, including going to conferences that are outside of your norm and reading articles from industries or businesses that are dissimilar to your startup. Search for magazines and books that are not part of your usual reading, too. What novel groups will you join? Online and in person—again, look to the unique and nontypical. Commit to reading some trendy blogs, listening to some new podcasts, and following different brands and people on Instagram (the ones you wouldn't usually). Why not read *Popular Mechanics* one day, or follow The Rock on Instagram? Or listen to the *Punch Up the Jam* or *Song Salad* podcasts? Try something that doesn't naturally appeal to you, and you'll be more likely to uncover a hidden treasure. All of these practices will help your brain and thoughts expand, which will translate into your mind wandering, thus enabling you to come up with more imaginative ideas.

Additionally, train your brain to avoid the everyday. You can do this in several ways, such as looking for new adventures and finding fresh ways of completing the tasks that you always perform. Try a trending workout (boxing ballet?), give a new restaurant a chance (Colorado cuisine?), and look under the rocks and get lost once in a while.

Last, another innovation-building practice is to write down five pie-in-the-sky ideas every day and see if there is any potential in them. You can pull new, ambitious ideas from anywhere, including all of the places I've just mentioned. The goal here is to dream bigger than your biggest competitor!

Relax

As counterintuitive as it may seem, you can become more innovative by relaxing more. Relaxation loosens the brain, so take a walk, meditate, practice yoga, and get out in nature. These activities will disrupt your logical thoughts, which is good because logic thwarts creativity.

Take a nap, too, because the more well rested you are, the better able you'll be to innovate and brainstorm. And we could all use a good nap, couldn't we, ladies?

Bond

We're creatures of habit and convenience, and most of us usually interact with those who are similar to ourselves; it's natural. However, when we associate with people who are unlike us, we expand our world and open new doors. We get fresh perspectives when we communicate with others from different backgrounds, personalities, and areas of expertise. I often run ideas by those who are the opposite of me to get a different point of view. It really works, so give it a try. It's also so amazingly cool to have different types of people in your life!

Experiment More

If you want to become extra innovative and disruptive, experiment more. Get out there and try new approaches and different ways of building and processing things (both at your business and in your home) through trial and error, simplifying tasks, and dismantling and updating standardized processes in a unique way. Always ask a lot of questions and observe as much as possible. Listen and watch instead of always jumping in. (This is a bit like being a mother: sometimes you just have to kick back and monitor what your kids do without interfering.)

It's also advantageous to solicit feedback, particularly from frontline employees and customers. They often see things from a better perspective. And, surprisingly, you actually become more innovative as you get older, due to your experience and the luck you've had with trying new tricks. So stick with your startup for a long time, and keep those birthdays coming!

Don't Wait

Pioneering women don't wait for opportunities, and you shouldn't either. Go out there and find them, and always turn your attention to the future. Remember that if you don't ask, you won't get what you're after. Don't stop pushing, and avoid the need to be perfect (as mentioned throughout this book). If you continue to strive for perfection, you'll lose speed, which is the name of the game when it comes to disruption as an entrepreneur. No one is perfect either—although you are all super amazing in your own way.

Innovate Every Day

Train yourself to make innovation a part of every day, by having an innovation plan and scheduling regular brainstorming sessions with your team. During these sessions, everyone should throw out ideas without anyone shooting any of them down, taking each one and building on it. You never know where you'll end up, and you can also invite outside people to join in on these idea-hashing activities. They will bring a fresh perspective since they are not as close to the work. If you are a solopreneur, perhaps you can team up with another fempreneur or business contact for these fun brain-storming meetups.

File It

Another best practice is to create a file on your laptop that's an innovation file. In it, you'll store random ideas that interest you, no matter how diverse. You can also collect all of your inspirations in an innovation journal instead.

As a next step, randomly match the ideas and try to find a way to make them work together—it's good practice for spotting opportunities in your everyday world. Think about and identify who will be your "person" to discuss these potential disruptions with—you'll need one—perhaps someone from your mastermind group.

Boosting Your Creative Thinking

For this Mindset Shift, you'll need more than innovative thinking. You should also strive to boost your creativity. Creativity and innovation are related, but there is a distinction between the two. Creativity is being able to see brand-new ideas or the connection between two things that are unrelated, whereas innovation is about transforming these ideas into products or processes. Creativity involves ideas, and innovation involves execution.

To become more creative, we just need to practice. It's like exercise, where we must build those creativity biceps to get stronger. Yup, another workout for you. The more we keep trying, the more creative we'll become, and creativity is vital for modern business owners.

Follow Best Practices

There are some best practices that you can leverage for bolstering creativity. Why not try to take a new route somewhere instead of continuing on the same one that you follow every day? Is there a business or store that you pass by all the time that you are curious about? Why not pop in? Find a really, really bad idea and then pick out the best parts of it. Start over with some task that you do all the time, and find a unique way to approach it as if it were your first day on the job. Think about it like disassembling something and then putting it together in a fresh way!

When working at your startup or formulating something original, if you take a break for a while and get some air or do something else, it will give you a lift. Set aside 30 minutes every day for creativity: you can paint, play piano, draw, or dance. This will tap into the creative part of your brain. If you're drawing or daydreaming, just let your ideas flow.

Learning new skills can help, too. Why not take classes, attend webinars, and read? I know there is something you've always been dying to learn how to do—maybe skydiving or studying another language. The sky's the limit, and you can even jump from it if you want while speaking French on the way down. I've gone indoor skydiving a few times, and I love it. It forces me to think totally differently. Maybe that is something you can try, too. And it's so much fun, whirling around in the air like that!

Stay Healthy

When it comes to your creativity, being healthy is a must. Ensure that you are getting enough sleep, because the more rest you get, the more creative you'll be. Drink lots of water as well, because water keeps you from feeling sluggish and improves brain function. Put an emphasis on incorporating breaks throughout your day and discover methods to relax. As mentioned, stress inhibits creativity, so include downtime in your schedule. That's when your inspiration builds up. It can also help to eat healthier by making good choices like salads, fruits, and vegetables. (It's good for you as well, so bring on the broccoli.)

Write It Down

Make a point to write more. Put together an article or journal at random without a particular focus. This habit boosts your creativity and also helps establish you as an expert (as discussed in Mindset Shift 5). Choose subjects that are outside of your wheelhouse (in addition to those that you know). That way you'll have to do research, you'll learn more, and you'll be forced to come up with a creative way to present your ideas.

Change the Ambience

Sometimes all it takes to become more creative is to change the atmosphere and mix it up. When you are in a different location, you are out of your comfort zone. If you work at home, perhaps you can sit outdoors or at a safe coworking space. I used to hit a French bakery here in town with extensive seating and good Wi-Fi to challenge my status quo (although I had to refrain from eating too many macaroons). Now, it is often just as simple as moving into a different room in my home.

Turn on some music for a change, as music can frustrate your logical thinking—rap, jazz, pop, whatever you're into. Write out your ideas with a pen and paper and get in there and use your hands. You can also isolate yourself so that you can think more clearly. Ensure that the process, whichever you settle on, is fun by making it a game. Laugh it up, too, because laughter is good for getting those creative juices flowing.

Perhaps you might even take things a step further and set up an inspirational spot in your startup or your home—think reading corner, she-shed, or creativity room. Although the she-shed didn't work out so well for Cheryl (it burned down in the State Farm commercial), I've always wanted one, don't you?

Above all else, give yourself some time to chill. Play Ping-Pong, take a breather, or go for a stroll. You can also move where you sit; even relocating across the room may give you the change in perspective you need. Let your mind wander. Daydream and see where your thoughts take you. When you give your brain a rest, a creative idea will often come to you subconsciously.

Brainstorm

You are a startup maven now, so keep pushing the edges to become more inspired all the time. Dedicate some time specifically each day for brainstorming by implementing a method for generating ideas, and making that a part of your routine. Reward yourself and others, too, for being creative. If you come up with a great idea, or someone else on your team does, treat them or yourself. It doesn't have to be anything big but enough to stimulate you to produce more ideas. Did someone say chocolate Frappuccino? Give a bonus for brilliance and for thinking outside of the box (even if it's just to yourself).

Stay Optimistic and Play Games

Remaining hopeful stimulates inspiration, so endeavor to look on the bright side and work on an attitude adjustment if necessary. There are also some creative-thinking exercises that you can do daily. Incorporate them and other brainstorming activities into your routine. Remember those drawing pages where the picture is half complete and you must finish it? Pick exercises like that from creative workbooks for adults, which are fun to do.

Other best practices include taking two unrelated subjects and finding a way to tie them together. Like oranges and snails, or butterflies and baseball. How can you connect them? There's always a way. When in doubt, sketch it out: go up to a white board and doodle. You can also perform word association games. If I say "successful," you say? Why, *you*, of course!

Develop a plan for how you'll incorporate some creative activity into your schedule. As part of that, decide how you'll add more writing (think thought-leadership pieces or reflective journaling) into your norm—you'll become a more disruptive and innovative leader as a result.

FINAL THOUGHTS

You are a budding business owner who must wrap your mind and hands around this Mindset Shift by building your resilience, learning to reinvent and rebrand frequently, and always striving to build your innovation and creativity while implementing it at your startup. Now is the time for you to go into growth mode. Let's close with the words of pioneering scientist Marian Diamond: "If you always do what you did, you'll always get what you got."[4] Get what you want and what you don't even know you want yet instead, fempreneur!

REBOOTING, REPEATING, AND AVOIDING BURNOUT ALONG THE WAY

n combination, all of the qualities and practices discussed throughout this book will help you develop an entrepreneurial mindset. You've made a great deal of progress, and your thought processes are morphing, so give yourself a pat on the back—you sure deserve it. Although you've done a lot of work, there's still more terrain to cover. The Mindset Shifts described in previous chapters must be continuously revisited, rebooted, and repeated in order to keep driving business advancement and growth. Additionally, you must simultaneously develop coping strategies for avoiding burnout and preventing feelings of overwhelm while continuing to grow and stretch.

When you are a fempreneur, you have to get comfortable with this revision practice as you tweak processes and pivot toward success. By committing to making the necessary Mindset Shifts repeatedly, both you and your business will thrive by activating and launching your inner entrepreneur.

Preventing Burnout

As you continue to repeat and reboot, the intense focus and drive to steer the ship forward brings the potential for getting burned out early. Burnout often results from being inundated—when you feel like you are being pulled in too many directions or when you just have too much to do and deal with. You'll recognize the feeling when it happens to you: you'll be sitting at your desk, staring blankly at your computer screen and knowing that you have a lot to complete, but yet you just feel frozen and unable to figure out what to do next because there is so much to do. Has that ever happened to you before? I bet. I've been there more than once myself.

You are more at risk for burnout as a business owner than ever before because we have more fluidity today than we did in the past. This is particularly true if you are a solopreneur and growing your company all by yourself. Your work is also more demanding as you are making sales, building your brand, dealing with production, filling orders, and more. Multiple stakeholders—clients, employees, and partners—need your attention 24/7, and the environment is constantly evolving, and that doesn't even include your other obligations to family, friends, and yourself. Did you hear the phrases "Mom, I can't find my [insert anything here]" and "I'm going to need to triple my order, and I need it tomorrow" within five minutes of each other? Welcome to my world.

As noted in a *Harvard Business Review* study, 25 percent of entrepreneurs feel moderately burned out at some point during their business career.[1] Some of the most common side effects reported in the study were panic attacks, anxiety, outbursts, extreme exhaustion, and disruptions in their home life. Further, research from Montreal University suggests that women are more prone to work burnout than men, and female business owners are at greater risk for burnout because of the multiple roles women play and the higher burden that falls on them compared to men in relation to housework and childcare—particularly if they are performing all of the roles associated with running the startup by themselves.[2]

Signs and Strategies

Some signs that burnout has already occurred include a general lack of energy or desire for accomplishment, as well as fatigue. Did you fall asleep on the couch with your laptop again last night? Yawn on a Zoom call in the face of an important prospect? Yikes! Additional symptoms can manifest in terms of reduced productivity and a lack of motivation. Burnout and overwhelm can lead to miscommunication, accidents, or trouble in our personal relationships due to our irritability and fatigue. Have you been responding too critically to emails or clients' demands? Find yourself saying things like "I've already told you that five times," or sighing audibly upon receiving hard-to-fulfill requests? Do you not feel like embarking on a juicy new project that's right up your alley? Oh my. These could be red flags.

Other warning signals associated with burnout include making mistakes, forgetting things, and lacking desire for what you used to love. Reversing and preventing burnout is an important part of this final fempreneurial Mindset Shift.

One way to deal with feeling burned out or inundated at your startup is to try to identify your major stressors and come up with a plan to address them. (Whether they're administrative tasks, order fulfillment, or your killjoy competitor, I hear you.) Catalog them on a sheet of paper and rank them from most stressful to least stressful. Then brainstorm about how you can eliminate or reduce each.

It can also help to simplify: declutter, ask for assistance, delegate, and do what you can to make your processes more streamlined. Have you thought about hiring a virtual assistant? Doing so can be life changing! Why not outsource some of your household chores? Who wants to spend time folding towels when they could be at the park enjoying a picnic with their family?

Also be sure to strive to lessen your anxiety. Get outdoors, take breaks, incorporate a fitness routine, and meditate, as we've talked about before. Being burned out is a signal that you need to rest more and find moderation in your life. It's important to get up from behind your desk and move around throughout the workday. As the leader of the company you need to know when more is less and when you should stop for the day and regroup.

To move away from feeling burned out, get into personal management, or the management of everything you do. Take control of both your commitments and actions and learn to organize. Put self-care at the top of your list by getting enough sleep, nutrition, and exercise. Doesn't a long bike ride followed by a healthy salad sound like heaven right about now? Go back to the time-management plans I talked about in Mindset Shift 4. Committing to taking steps to increase your work-life balance will reduce feelings of burnout and help you lead a more productive and happier life. You can have everything you want in your life and more, fempreneur! Be smart and manage it.

Ditch Being Overwhelmed

When we are constantly juggling (which is common for female business owners), our equilibrium can get knocked out of alignment. If there is a lack of stability, we can feel intensely overwhelmed, and if we are overwhelmed, we won't be able to move our startups forward.

The best method to reduce this sort of overwhelm is by setting clear goals and boundaries. Start by asking yourself some simple questions:

- Where do you *want* to spend your time?
- What are your priorities?
- What is unnecessarily sucking up your hours without providing a lot of value in return?
- How can your time be better allocated?
- Do you need to hire more people or outsource some tasks?

Based on your answers, make a few adjustments and communicate with the key people in your life to get their support (clients, friends, coworkers, and family members). Talk to your partner and family about what parts of the day you're dedicating to spend with them and what hours you're earmarking for the success of your startup (and yourself). Your needs matter, and you want to make this business thrive! Then, commit to your new schedule and you'll quickly see the positive effects of these changes. Go, girl!

You'll be revisiting the basics discussed earlier in this book and finding time for YOU: your health, fitness, and well-being. Watch a video, listen to a book, sit quietly and think, or hit the rowing machine . . . and always find happiness within your day—it's there if you look, so record and celebrate it. As I've mentioned, I have a journal that outlines the good things that are happening, and I love writing in it! It somehow makes them more real, or substantial, when you put them to paper, and there are always plenty of joyful moments when you seek them.

Celebrate the little wins and flashes of cheerfulness, and you'll feel your balance shift, a critical aspect of your overall mindset adjustment. Why not put on that new red dress and high heels and throw yourself a party? You deserve it because you are amazing! What's more, throw your hands up in the air in the direction of burnout. As author Thomas E. Rojo Aubrey said, "Dear Stress, I would like a divorce. Please understand it is not you, it is me."[3] Divorce your stress and anything else that is not serving you, fempreneur.

Engaging in Continuous Learning

Something else that will continue to be a part of your entrepreneurial journey is the adoption of a mindset reflective of constant learning and expansion. You must grow with your business. As your startup builds in success, your knowledge and presence must buoy with it as well. Rise to the occasion and grow your network, personal brand, and expertise to match. You are an even bigger deal now!

The higher profile you are, the more you will be out there showcasing your growth and abilities, so start participating in panels and contributing more to your field. Don't be afraid of these new opportunities or doubt yourself. You have worked hard for and deserve all that is coming your way. Also, endeavor to always acquire new skills: keep taking courses, attending conferences and webinars, and reading as if your life depends on it—because your continued business traction does.

You should be continuously updating your knowledge in several key areas, including industry trends, global developments, technological advances, and innovations, as well as your core area of expertise. It will also pay to get some certifications under your belt. There are many related to digital marketing and social media and others related to business basics; workshops also work well here. Some suggested courses and certifications include the following, many of which are free:

- YouTube's Certification
- Facebook's BluePrint Certification
- HubSpot Academy's Certification
- Google IT Support Professional
- Hootesuite's Social Marketing Certification

- Google Ads Certification
- Google Analytics IQ Certification
- Twitter Flight School Certification
- Google Digital Garage Certification
- HubSpot's Social Media Analytics Certification
- Bing Ads Certification
- Digital Marketing Institute's certifications

Also, look into getting more information related to standard business subjects, such as marketing, economics, accounting, finance, organizational behavior, business law, and more. Other topics that you can find some interesting courses on are crowdfunding, SEO, email marketing, leadership, and communication, among many others.

As mentioned in Mindset Shift 5, part of this continuous learning involves networking and joining in on the conversation in terms of what's going on in your field and what's to come. In addition to industry-specific groups (which you should most definitely join), there are some wonderful organizations out there specifically for women entrepreneurs, including these:

- National Association of Women Business Owners (NAWBO)
- American Business Women's Association
- Ladies Who Launch
- National Association for Female Executives
- Female Entrepreneur Association
- Ladies America

There are others aimed specifically at entrepreneurs (both women and men), including these:

- Young Entrepreneur Council (YEC)
- Small Giants Virtual Peer Groups
- Startup Nation

Some LinkedIn groups that you may find interesting (again, in addition to those related to your industry) include:

- Entrepreneurs Meet Investors
- Leadership Think Tank
- Future Trends

- Entrepreneurs Network
- A Startup Specialists Group
- On Startups
- Band of Entrepreneurs
- Bright Ideas and Entrepreneurs
- Digital Marketing

There are also some wonderful Facebook groups for fempreneurs, including the following two:

- Boss Babes Networking
- Women Helping Women Entrepreneurs

Stay up-to-date with what different experts are saying, and watch other companies in your industry as well. There will always be something to add, adjust to, absorb, copy, or otherwise embrace, so be sure to wrap your arms around this aspect of your entrepreneurial Mindset Shift. One thing about business and being a business owner is that it will never sit still. You have got to keep wiggling, hustling, and finding new and creative ways to reach customers and deal with competitors. In the words of Oprah Winfrey, "Don't worry about being successful but work toward being significant and the success will naturally follow."[4]

Knowing What to Avoid

As part of the repeat and reboot processes, being an effective female founder is not just about the things that you must do but also about the things you should avoid, and understanding this distinction is another vital aspect of your fempreneurial Mindset Shift. For starters, productive entrepreneurs avoid overscheduling. Although they make the most of their time by being focused and productive, they refrain from overcommitting to the point where they're not able to get anything done.

One simple rule of thumb I use to decide whether or not I will participate in additional tasks or obligations is to analyze whether my participation does anything to further my end goals (like those related to my business or brand) or means something to me personally. If not, I decline politely; you should, too. Fempreneurs are smart with their daily routine and focus on accomplishments vs. hours, and you are a smart fempreneur!

Thriving startup leaders also avoid mediocrity. They go big or go home, looking at life as a challenge and giving their all to those things they commit to. High-achieving moguls treat each new project and opportunity as if they are auditioning for their next big gig. So many times people have said to me, "You are so lucky. You get to do such cool things for work." I simply reply that these experiences weren't part of my day-to-day but merely opportunities that I created for myself or my business.

You, too, must find your own chances to shine. No one is going to hand them to you on a silver platter. Then, once you get them, execute upon them by going into full glow mode. The most effective business owners strive for quality and excellence in everything they do—and girl, you are no exception.

Successful women also avoid beating themselves up. You can't win 'em all. You have to embrace failure and learn from your mistakes, be open to feedback, and use each opportunity as a chance to improve. Masterful moguls understand that the more they fail, the more they'll ultimately prevail—it's part of the game. I've had plenty of setbacks, rejections, and points where I wondered if I was going in the right direction, but I didn't set up camp in them. I packed up my tent and found a new spot. You must too. Grab your gear and move on.

Last, prosperous entrepreneurs avoid avoidance. Execution is their sport, and they tackle things head-on, including tough conversations and challenges. They don't leave anything to chance. Thriving businesswomen are master communicators and are much more proactive than their less-profitable peers. Although it can be uncomfortable at times, being direct is the only way to obtain the information needed to get what they want. Their ability to anticipate and see opportunities and threats makes them action-oriented and highly valued leaders, and you are one of them.

What's more is that you will have to continue to reboot and repeat as the last part of your Mindset Shift. Reboot those areas of your business that have stalled or slowed down—unplug them, fix them, and start again as necessary. Although you will always be moving forward, you will have to take a step backward from time to time, and that's necessary and even to be expected. There will need to be upgrades in equipment, processes, software, and people, yourself included.

Then repeat. None of the steps that we have discussed in previous Mindset Shifts is "one and done." You will have to go back to them and refresh, reprise, rebuild, and do them all over again. Developing the right mindset comes about with taking action and becoming a true fempreneur—by embracing your USP; identifying opportunities; and then making them happen through research, planning, goal setting, and execution. After that, you'll embrace your entrepreneurial attitude, developing the grit, confidence, and tenacity to kick your hustle into overdrive.

You must also make adjustments to the way you budget and deal with money, and learn to get the most out of your time for maximum productivity, happiness, and effectiveness. The entire time, you'll be working on building your presence, networking, and establishing yourself as a thought leader, while growing your brand on social as you increase awareness.

You'll also be cultivating mad leadership skills and guiding your team to achieve greatness, all while overcoming obstacles with resilience, innovating and rebranding as necessary along the way. The path of an entrepreneur is not an easy one; however, if you are committed to making the necessary Mindset Shifts, both you and your business will thrive. You've got this, girl! Go make it happen.

FINAL THOUGHTS

Someone once said, "If you don't have big dreams and goals, you'll end up working for someone who does." Fempreneur, you've got lofty dreams and goals, so I know that won't be you! Throughout this book, you have been learning about the Mindset Shifts necessary to develop as a flourishing business owner. If you walk away without taking anything else from this book, I want you to know that you can do whatever you put your mind to. It is all about your outlook and shifting in terms of each of the 10 areas I've discussed:

1. Taking action
2. Embracing an entrepreneurial attitude
3. Cultivating financial confidence
4. Organizing your time
5. Branding and building presence
6. Getting social by mastering social media basics
7. Staying social by leveraging social media options
8. Leading your startup
9. Going into growth mode
10. Repeating, rebooting and avoiding burnout along the way

Review and revisit these areas often. Complete the Fempreneur Action Plan at the end of this book, and then redo the exercises when you feel that you are waning in any of the areas. You are going to be getting grittier and savvier all the time, but adjusting your mindset also takes continuous work. And I know that you are willing to do the work. You are an amazing fempreneur who's in charge of her dreams, earnings, potential, and life.

Along your entrepreneurial journey, always remember why you started and how much you've grown! When you need an extra push or someone to talk to, you can set up some time with me for mentoring on my website: www.charlenewalters.com. I'd love to help. In the meantime, adjust your crown and repeat, because there is no stopping you now that you have launched your inner entrepreneur!

A LETTER FROM ME TO YOU

Dear Fempreneur,

You are not powerless!
You are not alone!
You are in control of your earnings and your life!
You have got what it takes and can do whatever you set your mind to!
You are smart and capable!
You *are a fempreneur* and will be successful!
You're able to research your target audience; plan; and organize your time, finances, marketing, and business strategy!
You can stay on top of your schedule and productivity!
You know what to do to eliminate negative self-talk and self-sabotage!
You understand how to pivot and adjust when you hit setbacks!
You know how to utilize social media to grow your brand and your presence!
You can address naysayers and lead your company with the best of them!
You are able to network and brand yourself and your business!
You are confident, gritty, and innovative!
There is no stopping you!
You deserve this!
You have developed a true entrepreneurial mindset and will lead your startup to success!
Go out there and make it happen, fempreneur!

I believe in you,

FEMPRENEUR ACTION PLAN

Business Concept and Planning Worksheet (Mindset Shift 1)

In Mindset Shift 1, you learned a lot about what it takes to become a successful fempreneur by taking action. Whether you've already launched your own business or are just getting started, you can benefit from completing this business planning activity. Doing so will help you to fine-tune your products and services, processes, and target market—and will also enable you to perfect your messaging and customer acquisition approaches, which is a large part of your entrepreneurial success and Mindset Shift.

What Is Your Business Concept?

What are your interests?

What are your skills?

What are you passionate about?

What type of business would you like to start or do you already have?

How can you incorporate your skills, passion, interests, and expertise into your business?

What is the demand for your product or service?

Who are your main competitors?

What market share do they already have? How much can you expect to realistically gain?

What Is Your USP (Unique Selling Proposition)?

What problem exists with other products or services in your space?

How does (or will) your product or service address that problem? What solution will it provide?

What makes it different from other products or services already on the market?

What is your business niche?

How Will You Conduct Market Research?

What method will you use—for example, surveys, focus groups, interviews, or something else?

What questions will you ask?

How will you find and reach participants—in person, online, through a research company or partner?

What type of competitive and industry analysis will you conduct?

What are your plans for creating an MVP (minimum viable product) or improving your product if you already have one?

Who Is Your Target Audience?

What are the demographics of the people you are trying to reach? Include age, gender, race, income, geographical location, and other factors.

What are their psychographic and lifestyle characteristics (e.g., interests, hobbies, lifestyle, habits)?

What related products or services are they currently buying? What are their pain points with the products or services that they are currently buying?

What messaging will appeal to them?

Where do they congregate—both online and in person?

How will you or do you reach them?

Any other relevant information?

Will You Start as a Side Hustle?

Will you start your business as a side hustle? Have you already started?

How much time do you have to devote to your business in the next six months?

Do you already have a business plan? If not, when will you complete it?

Do you have a mentor? If not, who will help you review your business concepts?

What hours and days will you or do you devote to your business?

How much do you hope to make by the end of the first year? Or if you're already in business, in your next year?

What steps will you take to launch your business? Or if you've already launched it, what steps will you take to grow it?

What are your long-term goals, and how long will it take for you to get there?

Who can help you?

What resources do you already have?

What resources do you need to obtain?

What is your plan for funding? How will you obtain funds to grow your business?

Website Development

Do you already have a website? If not, what hosting site will you use?

What information will you include on your website? What will you add or adjust if you already have one?

Do you have a business name, logo, and graphics you can use? Do you need more?

How will customers reach you? What will you use for contact information? Have you been getting a lot of hits? If not, what can you do to pivot?

Will you incorporate ecommerce? Have you already done so?

How will you solicit and utilize customer testimonials? Do you need to update them on your website?

Any other bells and whistles to include or add to your site?

Do you have your business social media accounts and pages set up? If not, when will you do so? Do you need to update anything there?

What Is Your Sales Plan?

What are your sales goals for the next six months? The next year? Five years?

How many calls or contacts do you need to make per day to achieve those goals?

What days and times will you devote to making calls/outreach attempts?

What is your sales script? What do you or will you say to potential customers?

What are some possible objections that you might, or do you already, encounter?

What do you, or can you, say to overcome those objections?

Do you have any fears related to selling?

What can you do, or have you done, to address and overcome those fears?

Who can you practice or fine-tune your pitching with?

Fempreneur Action Plan: Attitude Enhancement Exercise (Mindset Shift 2)

In Mindset Shift 2, you read about the second phase of the Mindset Shift necessary for fempreneurs: embracing an entrepreneurial attitude through committing to your venture for the long haul and developing grit. I described many ways you can do this, including paying your dues, tapping into passion and perseverance, embracing risk taking, dealing with haters, boosting your confidence, and overcoming impostor syndrome and self-sabotage. The following attitude enhancement exercise will help guide you through this Mindset Shift as you hone your grit and tenacity via those methods, no matter what stage of the entrepreneurial journey you're at.

Embracing an Attitude of High Quality and Service

How will you, or do you, serve customers?

What steps will you, or do you, take to listen to them attentively?

How will you, or do you, track and follow up with those things that you say you will? What method will you, or do you, use to do so?

What will you, or do you, do to provide a high level of quality and service at your business?

How will you, or do you, build rapport with your clients? Is there anything that you can do to improve in this regard?

Developing Passion and Grit

What are you passionate about related to your business?

How long will it take to get your business to the level of thriving? Or if it's already there, what will you do to take it to the next level?

What will you do to practice developing grit?

What time will you make for skill building and developing grit? How will you incorporate it into your daily routine?

How will you focus and check in on your business goals? What do you want to accomplish long term, and how long will it take for you to get there?

What do you want to learn, and how much time will you devote to mastering it? When and how often?

Do you know any really gritty people? How can you spend more time with them?

What will you do to think like a queen?

How comfortable are you with taking risks?

What type of risks are you committed to taking? (Remember to push yourself here.)

How will you get more adept at getting out of your comfort zone?

Do you have any haters in your life? How will you, or do you, deal with them? What can you, or do you, say to combat their negativity?

Increasing Confidence

How confident are you? What are some areas that you need to work on?

Are you in a women's mastermind group? If so, how can you improve or get more out of it? If not, who might you invite to form one?

What's the "why" behind your business? Why did you, or will you, start a business?

What do you want? How will you measure your milestones on the way to achieving it?

What are those things that you love about yourself? What makes you awesome? Brag here!

How will you, or do you, gather feedback when you hit a setback or experience a rejection of some sort? What will you, or do you, say?

What are some sources of energy for you when you hit an obstacle (e.g., connecting with friends, exercising, reading, watching a movie)?

Who is, or will be, your ups-and-downs buddy to cheer you up if you experience a business letdown?

How will you, or do you, celebrate both your successes and your failures?

Dealing with Impostor Syndrome/Self-Sabotage

Do you suffer from impostor syndrome or self-sabotage? How so?

What affirming mantra will you, or do you, say to yourself when negative internal dialogue creeps in?

Do you already have, or will you create, a journal for chronicling the positive things happening in your business and life? What are some of those things currently?

How can you, or do you, pull yourself up when you experience self-doubt?

Who can you, or do you, talk to about negative feelings related to your abilities and yourself (someone you trust who will help you stay positive)?

Fempreneur Action Plan: Money Mindset Plan and Budget (Mindset Shift 3)

In Mindset Shift 3, you got a lot of information about making the transformation to fempreneur, which involves cultivating financial confidence. This money mindset plan and budgeting activity will help you no matter what phase of business you're in. Completing it will allow you to analyze your current thoughts related to money, remove potential blocks and fears, set financial targets and goals, and get more comfortable talking about money. It will also enable you to improve your financial situation by conducting a spending analysis, creating a better budget, and setting financial targets and goals for both yourself and your business.

Current Money Mindset

What comes to mind when you think about money?

What did your parents say to you about money when you were growing up? How did they treat it and approach spending?

Do you consider yourself good with money? Why or why not?

How confident are you that you will have a positive financial future? What can you do to improve your outlook?

What mental blocks or fears (if any) do you have related to money?

Are you currently living paycheck to paycheck? If so, how can you turn that around?

What debt do you have, including credit cards, bills, loans, mortgage, other?

What can you do to help eliminate/reduce these debts?

Do you have any items that you can sell to bring in more money? What are they, and where or how will you sell them?

Improving Your Money Mindset

Are you comfortable talking about money?

How can you improve your comfort level when discussing money and your finances?

What can you do to learn to say no to those things that are not within your budget or avoid peer pressure related to spending?

Do you deserve to have a lot of money? Why or why not?

How will you give yourself permission to become rich?

What will you do to change your attitude and learn to love money?

What negative words associated with money do you use? What steps will you take to eliminate them from your vocabulary?

What's your new money mantra? For example, "I attract money" or "I deserve to have financial success." How will you incorporate this mantra into your daily routine?

Spending Analysis

What are your current expenses? Break them down according to your four walls (food, shelter, utilities, transportation) and other areas.

What else are you spending money on? Look at your recent banking statements and accounts to find out.

Which expenses are necessary?

Which expenses are unnecessary?

What is the total amount of your current expenses?

What is your current income (all sources)?

Are you spending more than you are making? By what amount?

What do your savings and investment accounts look like? What can you tweak here?

What areas can you improve on in terms of your spending?

What are your financial targets? What areas do you want to change?

What are some SMART goals to achieve these targets?

What are your short-term financial goals—i.e., in the next six to twelve months?

What are your long-term financial goals—i.e., in five years? Ten years?

What microsteps will you take to achieve these goals?

Business Budget

What are the necessary expenses related to your business? How much do they add up to?

What are some business expenses that you can reduce or eliminate? What methods will you use to reduce them?

What revenue is your business generating or do you plan for it to generate within the next year? Five years? Ten years?

What does your bottom line look like, and what can you do to improve it?

Where might you be able to eliminate or reduce critical costs, and how will you do so?

What does your new or desired budget look like?

What will you do to enhance your negotiation skills?

Where will you look for additional sources of funding when needed? How will you prepare?

What are your financial targets related to your business? What areas do you want to change?

What are some SMART goals to achieve these targets?

What are your short-term goals related to your business's financial situation— i.e., for the next six to twelve months?

What are your long-term goals related to your business's financial situation— i.e., for the next five years? Ten years?

What microsteps will you take to achieve these goals?

What will you do to instill a cost-cutting culture and mindset within your business?

How often will you review your spending and when?

Fempreneur Action Plan: Work-Life Balance and Time-Management Goal Setting (Mindset Shift 4)

In Mindset Shift 4, you learned all about how to schedule and maximize your time by setting goals, managing your minutes more efficiently and effectively, and achieving a better work-life balance. As business owners, caretakers, and more, women particularly need help in this area. Completing this exercise will empower you to take control of your time and ensure better work-life balance, which are both critical aspects of your entrepreneurial Mindset Shift. Getting this right will help you (and your business) grow and thrive.

Goal Setting

What are your top 10 *business* goals? Be sure to make them SMART goals.

Where will you set up your action plans related to these goals (e.g., in a journal or on your laptop perhaps)? Remember to include information about responsibilities, resources, timelines, and the microsteps for making them happen.

What's your plan for identifying and creating an action plan template?

Where will you store and organize your action plans?

What are your top 10 *personal* goals?

Where and how will you set up and complete your action plans related to these goals (e.g., calendar, laptop, journal)? Remember to include information about responsibilities, resources, timelines, and the microsteps for making them happen.

What will you name your master list (e.g., "Mary's Must Do's" or "Donna's Dealmakers")?

How will you track progress toward your goals? How often? What type of reminders will you use?

How will you check in on scheduled deadlines?

How will you break down and organize your goals in terms of the big picture vs. day-to-day plans?

Checklists and Daily Action Plans

How will you utilize checklists?

How and where will you organize the checklists?

What type of template will you use for your daily action plan? Have you already created it? If not, when will you do so?

How will you schedule your day, and what tool will you use?

What times will you dedicate as working "chunks" in your schedule (for example, 1–4 p.m. or 10–11 a.m. and 2–3 p.m.)?

How and when will you incorporate breaks? Lunch?

What will be your goal start and stop time for each day?

What tiny slots will you schedule throughout the day for checking in on your progress?

Organizing Your Time

Critically assess your current schedule: what are you spending the bulk of your time on?

Where are your time sucks (those things that take up a lot of time without providing a lot of value in return)?

What's distracting you?

Are there any holes in your schedule that you can better utilize?

What hours will you devote to your business?

What hours will you devote to other areas?

How will you minimize or eliminate distractions?

When will you eat and have snacks? Drink water?

Where will you store your daily schedule? What will you do to ensure that you are scheduling everything in your day?

Work-Life Balance

How many hours of sleep do you need each night? What is your plan for a sleep schedule? For example, when will you get up each morning and when will you go to bed?

What is important for you to make time for besides your business? How will you fit these things into your schedule?

Who's important for you to make time for? How will you do so?

What will you do to keep fit (exercise, yoga, fitness routines, something else)?

What are some things that you'll do to stay healthy?

What else will you do/incorporate to take care of your mind and soul?

What are some other obligations that must stay in your schedule?

Are you overcommitted? What are some things that you can say no to and remove from your schedule?

What can you do to outsource certain tasks or duties and/or get help?

What else can you do to take better control of your schedule?

What safeguards will you put in place to ensure that you are achieving better work-life balance?

How will you hold yourself accountable for your balance?

Fempreneur Action Plan: Branding and Presence-Building Plan (Mindset Shift 5)

In Mindset Shift 5, you acquired knowledge to help you with branding and building presence. As a fempreneur, you'll want to hone your personal brand, establish yourself as a thought leader, network, and increase visibility. Working on this branding and presence-building plan will help you to do so and master this portion of your entrepreneurial Mindset Shift. You can achieve all that you set your heart and mind to—and so much more!

Personal Branding

List three to four keywords for your personal brand.

What are your values and passions?

What is your value proposition? What do you have to offer that sets you apart from others in the same space?

What is your three- to four-sentence elevator pitch that you can use to describe yourself?

What do you want to be known for?

Who is your personal branding idol? How can you emulate her?

What are your top two to three goals related to personal branding, and what microsteps will you take to make them happen?

Networking

What professional associations will you join or do you already belong to?

What online groups will you join—on Facebook, LinkedIn, others?

How will you become more active in these groups?

How will you connect with influencers? Identify five influencers you will start interacting with.

What industry publications will you, or do you already, follow or subscribe to?

In what ways will you, or do you already, provide value to those in your network?

Building Visibility

What methods will you use—or are you currently using—to establish yourself as a thought leader? Will you blog or write articles? Do you already?

How will you, or do you, contribute to media outlets?

Will you, or have you already, written a book? If not, what might you write about, and when do you plan to do so?

How will, or does, speaking figure into your thought-leadership plan? What topics would you most like to talk about?

Are you interested in podcasting? Will you launch a podcast, or do you already have one? What podcasts will you listen to for inspiration?

Do you have your own website? If so, how will you showcase your thought leadership on it? If not, when will you create one?

What is your biggest dream related to thought leadership and personal branding? What steps can you take to turn that dream into a reality?

What are your top five goals related to building visibility, and what microsteps will you take to make them happen?

Fempreneur Action Plan: Visual Brand Style Guide (Mindset Shift 6)

In Mindset Shift 6, you were armed with the tips you need to master social media basics, including paying attention to consistency and quality, following and adhering to social media trends, and ensuring that you thwart and correct social media churn. In order to consistently put your best foot forward on social media, stick with brand messaging, and crank out content that will resonate with your target audience. This exercise will empower you to create a visual brand style guide as a road map to accomplish those goals.

Brand Mission and Values

What is your business's mission?

What is your business's vision?

What are the core values associated with your startup?

What do you stand for and hope to communicate?

What do you want to be known for?

Who is your target audience, and what type of content speaks to them?

Where do your target customers congregate on social media—i.e., which platforms?

What days and times are they most active on social media?

Aesthetics

Do you have a logo? If not, when will you create one? What does it, or will it, look like?

What guidelines will you implement in relation to the use of your logo?

What colors should be used in your brand communications? Include RGB, CMYK, and Pantone information for each.

What fonts or typography should be used in your brand communications? Include fonts, styles, sizes, and weights.

Messaging and "Feel"

What are some keywords that describe your brand and will be central to your messaging on social media and for all of your marketing communications?

What guidelines will you associate with the use of photos and images, or do you already?

How will you incorporate or infuse humor into your content?

What will you do to showcase social concerns and charitable affiliations in your content?

What will your messaging on social media be like? What messages do you want to convey?

Have you created customer personas for each of your customer segments? If not, when will you do so, and what will you name them?

What methods will you use to foster brand awareness?

What methods will you use to grow your followers/customer base?

What will you do to showcase your authentic brand personality?

What other suggestions do you have to inform your social media content and strategies?

Fempreneur Action Plan: Social Media Strategy Worksheet (Mindset Shift 7)

In Mindset Shift 7, we discussed the major social media platforms and how you can leverage them as a fempreneur: Instagram, Twitter, LinkedIn, Facebook, TikTok, Snapchat, Pinterest, and YouTube. You'll use them to network, build brand awareness and reach, and drive growth and conversions as a critical aspect of Mindset Shift 7 and your ultimate success as a business owner. Completing this worksheet will help you further solidify this process, no matter what stage of the entrepreneurial journey you're at.

Instagram Strategy

What is your username?

What information, links, and call to action will you include in your bio?

Which profile picture will you use? Is it consistent with your other profiles?

What is your theme (e.g., playful, feminine, professional, something else)?

What colors, filters, and fonts will you use?

How often will you post? When?

What types of content will you post?

How will you pull followers in and increase engagement?

What methods will you use to grow your followers?

What competitors will you look at for inspiration?

What are your goals related to Instagram?

Identify popular hashtags for your product and industry.

Who are some Instagram influencers that you should follow and engage with?

Will you run any paid ads on Instagram? If so, when and how often?

What's your strategy for tracking and improving metrics on this platform?

Twitter Strategy

What is your Twitter handle?

What information, links, and call to action will you include in your bio?

Which profile picture and banner will you use? Are they consistent with your other profiles?

What will you use as your pinned tweet?

How often will you post? When?

What types of content will you post?

How will you infuse humor in your posts?

How will you pull followers in and increase engagement?

What methods will you use to grow your follower base?

What competitors will you look at for inspiration?

What are your goals related to Twitter?

Identify popular hashtags for your product and industry.

Who are some Twitter influencers that you should follow and engage with?

What are your strategies for sharing blog and article posts on Twitter?

How will you use Twitter lists?

Will you run any paid ads on Twitter? If so, when and how often?

What's your strategy for tracking and improving metrics on this platform?

LinkedIn Strategy

Have you set up your personal profile on LinkedIn? Have you updated your summary and other important information?

Have you created your business page and set up the "About Us" section?

Which pictures will you use? Are they consistent with your other profiles?

What networking groups will you join?

How often will you post? When?

What types of content will you post?

Will you publish articles directly on LinkedIn?

How will you increase your connections and drive traffic to your business page and personal profile?

What competitors will you look at for inspiration?

What are your goals related to LinkedIn?

Identify popular hashtags for your product and industry.

Who are some LinkedIn influencers that you should follow and engage with?

What are your strategies for sharing blog and article posts on LinkedIn?

Will you run any paid or sponsored ads on LinkedIn? If so, when and what types?

What's your strategy for tracking and improving metrics on this platform?

Facebook Strategy

What is your Facebook username?

Have you created a page for your brand?

Which profile picture will you use? Is it consistent with your other profiles?

What will you use as your pinned post?

How often will you post? When?

What types of content will you post?

How will you infuse humor and your brand personality in your posts?

How will you pull followers in and increase engagement?

What methods will you use to grow friends and followers?

What competitors will you look at for inspiration?

What are your goals related to Facebook?

Identify popular hashtags for your product and industry.

Who are some Facebook influencers that you should follow and engage with?

What are your strategies for sharing blog and article posts on Facebook?

What are some Facebook groups that you can join and use to increase networking and build influence?

Will you run any paid ads on Facebook? If so, when and how often?

What's your strategy for tracking and improving metrics on this platform?

TikTok Strategy

Does this platform make sense for your brand? If so, what is your TikTok username?

Which profile picture will you use? Is it consistent with your other profiles?

How often will you create TikTok videos? When?

What types of content will you post (e.g., duets, challenges, duels, dances)?

How will you infuse humor in your posts?

How will you pull followers in and increase engagement?

What methods will you use to grow your followers?

What competitors will you look at for inspiration?

What are your goals related to TikTok?

Identify popular hashtags for your product/industry.

Who are some TikTok influencers that you should follow and engage with?

Will you run any paid ads on TikTok? If so, when and what type?

What's your strategy for tracking and improving metrics on this platform?

Snapchat Strategy

Does this platform make sense for your brand? If so, what is your Snapchat username?

Which profile picture will you use? Is it consistent with your other profiles?

How often will you snap? When?

What types of content will you snap?

How will you infuse humor in your snaps?

How will you pull followers in and increase engagement?

What methods will you use to grow your followers?

What competitors will you look at for inspiration?

What are your goals related to Snapchat?

Who are some Snap influencers that you should follow and engage with?

Will you run any paid ads on Snapchat? If so, when and how often?

What's your strategy for tracking and improving metrics on this platform?

Pinterest Strategy

Does this platform make sense for your brand?

What will your board names be and consist of?

How often will you pin? When?

What types of content will you pin?

Have you integrated your Etsy, YouTube, and Instagram accounts?

How will you increase engagement with your boards and pins?

How will you use rich pins?

What competitors will you look at for inspiration?

What are your goals related to Pinterest?

Who are some Pinterest influencers that you should follow and engage with?

Will you incorporate any paid advertising? If so, when and how?

What's your strategy for tracking and improving metrics on this platform?

YouTube Strategy

Have you already created your YouTube channel? Have you named it?

Which profile picture will you use? Is it consistent with your other profiles?

How often will you post and create new videos? When?

What tools will you use to identify keywords and commonly searched for phrases? What are some for your industry and products?

How will you use hooks in your videos as well as cover photos?

How will you increase followers and engagement?

What competitors will you look at for inspiration?

What are your goals related to YouTube?

What types of videos will you create?

Who are some YouTube influencers that you should follow and engage with?

Will you incorporate any paid advertising? If so, when and how?

What's your strategy for tracking and improving metrics on this platform?

Fempreneur Action Plan: Leadership and Skills-Building Exercise (Mindset Shift 8)

After reading Mindset Shift 8, you now know a lot more about what it takes to become a strong fempreneurial leader through developing your leadership traits, directing with empathy, incorporating flexibility, managing remote teams, and showing gratitude to your employees. This exercise will help you fine-tune these lessons and incorporate them into your daily startup leadership activities.

Leadership Skills

How would you rate your leadership skills on a scale of 1 to 10? What areas could you improve on?

In what way do you, or will you, communicate regularly with your team? What can you do to improve in this regard?

Do you lead with your heart or your mind? How so? What can you do to foster that balance?

What soft skills do you need to improve? At which do you excel?

How can you, or do you, put your employees' needs above your own?

How well do you delegate your work? What can you do to improve?

In what ways do you, or will you, provide guidance to your employees? Is there more you can or will do?

How do you, or can you, recognize and reward employee efforts at your startup?

Leadership Personality and Role Models

Have you taken a personality test? If not, when will you do so?

What is your personality type?

How does your personality type impact your leadership style?

What are your strengths as a leader? How can you capitalize on them?

What are your weaknesses as a leader? What can you do to improve them (e.g., taking courses, reading leadership books, or meeting with a coach)?

Who is your leadership role model? What do you like about her?

What can you do to emulate your role model?

How can you be, or are you, a role model to others on your team?

Staffing and Managing Your Team

How do you, or will you, incorporate flexibility for your staff?

Do you currently offer unlimited paid time off? If not, will you consider it?

Do you manage any remote employees? If not, will you offer remote working opportunities?

How will you measure, or do you measure, milestones and productivity for remote employees?

What expectations do you have, or will you establish, for remote workers? How will you communicate those?

How frequently will you, or do you, touch base with your employees?

Gratitude and Empathy

What are you currently doing, or will you do, to incorporate gratitude activities into your day-to-day routine?

Have you started using a gratitude journal? If not, will you? Will you encourage your employees to do the same?

What type of team-building activities are you using, or will you use, to help your team with bonding?

What else will you, or do you already, do to foster thankfulness?

What example do you set for your team, if you have one?

In what ways do you, or will you, pay it backward and give it forward?

What practices will you implement, or have you already implemented, to lead with empathy?

Fempreneur Action Plan: Resilience and Setback Survival Exercise (Mindset Shift 9)

In Mindset Shift 9, you learned a great deal about resilience, rebranding, reinvention, and boosting your innovation and creativity. This exercise will be useful to you when you experience a setback, in order to help you survive and become more resilient. The Patience and Resilience Prompts and Help sections will assist you in getting prepared before any obstacles come your way.

Resilience Prompts and Help

What type of resilience prompts can you put in your office environment?

What other resilience cues can you incorporate in your daily routine?

Who will be your "innovation ride or dies" whom you can run new ideas past?

What will be your go-to coping strategy when you encounter a setback or obstacle?

Have you encountered any big setbacks in the past? What were they?

What helped you get through previous obstacles, and how might you use that when you hit other setbacks?

Patience

What makes you impatient?

How will you practice patience?

Do you find yourself improving? How long did it take you to get there?

Resilience Plan

So you've hit a setback. What will you do now?

What are your Plans B, C, D, E, and F?

What are the next steps associated with your plan?

How will you execute those steps? What additional resources do you need?

How will you identify the problem associated with the obstacle and solve it?

Who will you ask questions of to better understand what occurred?

Why did this problem or setback occur?

How can you focus on the solution vs. the problem?

What are some possible fixes? Brainstorm and ensure that you have several ideas.

How will you reduce distractions so that you can execute your new plan?

Is there a silver lining here for you to uncover?

How can you get unstuck?

What are some tough questions to ask about how to proceed?

What may be newly possible now that wasn't before? Try to imagine something better.

How might you reframe the situation and put a positive spin on it?

How will you address and release negative feelings associated with this obstacle?

Have you put progress check-ins and reminders associated with your new plan on your calendar?

What will you do to thwart thinking negatively about this setback?

Fempreneur Action Plan: Entrepreneurial Plan for Rebooting and Growth (Mindset Shift 10)

Mindset Shift 10 taught you about preventing burnout, recognizing what to avoid, incorporating continuous learning, rebranding, and the need to constantly reboot and repeat. This exercise will help you thwart burnout and come up with a strategy for continuous learning and growth so that you can keep pushing your startup forward and enhance your entrepreneurial Mindset Shift.

Preventing Burnout

What are some warning signs of burnout? Have you experienced any?

Have you been responding to others too critically or getting frustrated easily?

Have you been making mistakes or forgetting important things?

Have you thought about hiring a virtual assistant?

What might you do to further delegate or streamline your responsibilities, tasks, or processes?

What will you do to ensure that you incorporate breaks throughout your day?

What are you doing in terms of self-care (e.g., sleep, fitness, meditation)? What can you do to improve here?

Where do you want to spend your time?

What are some methods that you can utilize to destress?

Continuous Learning Plan

What certificates will you pursue?

What virtual conferences will you attend?

What industry books and publications will you keep up with?

Which LinkedIn groups will you join?

Which Facebook groups will you join?

What courses will you enroll in?

Which professional associations will you become a member of?

What else will you do to keep learning?

How often will you revisit each phase of your fempreneurial Mindset Shift?

What else do you need to do to ensure your success? What steps will you take to make it happen?

Will you set up an appointment with a mentor to help you when you are stuck or need strategic advice? (It's a good practice once or twice a year.)

Is there anything holding you back? If so, how will you eliminate it and keep pushing forward?

Always remember, you are a fempreneur. With the right mindset and through your continued effort, you'll make it happen. Go for it!

ACKNOWLEDGMENTS

Many people have inspired me, listened to me, and guided me on the journey to launch this book. I am ever so grateful to the entire McGraw-Hill Professional team, particularly my editors, Cheryl Segura, Ruth Mills, and Amy Li, who believed in *Launch Your Inner Entrepreneur* and helped bring it to life. I am also thankful for my agent, Suzy Evans, and the Sandra Dijkstra Literary Agency, who have been wonderful to work with; my friend Robin Madell, who was an enormous help with formulating the book's proposal; Vanessa Campos, Bill Shaw, Jason Feifer, Terry Rice, and the rest of the *Entrepreneur* magazine team for their inspiration and support; Jon Steinberg of Cheddar; Barbara Cave Henricks and Pam Peterson of Cave Henricks Communications; John Honeycutt for his insight; and my friend Gail Summerskill and my mom, who have both served as overall sounding boards throughout the process.

Sending lots of love to all of the friends and family who've indulged me in many lengthy book conversations (too many to single out); my fellow writer friends and entrepreneur colleagues; and particularly my two amazing daughters, Avery and Tegan, who patiently tolerated my many nights and weekends in writing and editing mode at the laptop. Wishing the best of luck to my sister Michelle, who after being furloughed due to COVID-19, will begin the next chapter and her own fempreneurial journey.

Finally, I am forever indebted to you, the readers—current and future entrepreneurs. You are my true inspiration, going out there every day, hustling and making a difference for yourselves and your families. Thank you for your support, and in return, I'm sending lots of it right back at you. You've got this!

NOTES

Mindset Shift 1

1. Michael J. McManus, "Get the Facts on Women Business Owners," July 5, 2017, U.S. Department of Labor, https://blog.dol.gov/2017/07/05/get-facts-women-business-owners; "2019 State of the Women-Owned Businesses Report," *American Express*, last modified 2019, https://s1.q4cdn.com/692158879/files/doc_library/file/2019-state-of-women-owned-businesses-report.pdf; Rieva Lesonsky, "The State of Women Entrpreneurs," *Score*, March 24, 2020, https://www.score.org/blog/state-women-entrepreneurs.
2. "The 'Broken Rung' is the Biggest Obstacle Women Face," LeanIn.org, 2019, https://leanin.org/women-in-the-workplace-2019.
3. Julie Kashen, "How COVID-19 Sent Women's Workforce Progress Backward," *Center for American Progress*, October 30, 2020, https://www.americanprogress.org/issues/women/reports/2020/10/30/492582/covid-19-sent-womens-workforce-progress-backward.
4. Katty Kay and Claire Shipman, *The Confidence Code* (New York: Harper Collins, 2014), xii.
5. "2020 Trends for Women in Business," *Guidant Financial Reports,* https://www.guidantfinancial.com/small-business-trends/women-in-business/.
6. "Over 44 Million Americans Have a Side Hustle," *Bank Rate*, last modified 2017, https://www.bankrate.com/pdfs/pr/20170712-Side-Hustles.pdf.
7. "Study: Side Hustles and the Gender Pay Gap," *The Ascent*, December 6, 2019, https://www.fool.com/the-ascent/research/side-hustles/.
8. Michael T. Deane, "Top 6 Reasons New Businesses Fail," *Investopedia,* updated February 28, 2020, https://www.investopedia.com/financial-edge/1010/top-6-reasons-new-businesses-fail.aspx.
9. Monique Lhuillier Quotes, BrainyQuote.com, https://www.brainyquote.com/authors/monique-lhuillier-quotes.
10. Sara Blakely Quotes, BrainyQuote.com, https://www.brainyquote.com/quotes/sara_blakely_421753.
11. Sarah Berger, "Glossier: How This 33-Year-Old Turned Her Beauty Blog into a $1 Billion Brand," CNBC.com, March 20, 2019, https://www.cnbc.com/2019/03/20/how-emily-weiss-took-glossier-from-beauty-blog-to-1-billion-brand.html.
12. Eleanor Roosevelt, Goodreads Quotable Quote, Goodreads.com, https://www.goodreads.com/quotes/319111-it-takes-as-much-energy-to-wish-as-it-does.
13. Mia Hamm, Goodreads Quotable Quote, Goodreads.com, https://www.goodreads.com/quotes/185467-the-backbone-of-success-is-hard-work-determination-good-planning-and.

14. Gary Stockton, "Statistics and Obstacles Facing Women Entrepreneurs," *Experian Small Business News,* January 29, 2018, https://www.experian.com/blogs/small-business-matters/2018/01/29/statistics-and-obstacles-facing-women-entrepreneurs/.

15. Jennifer Brozic, "Nearly 1 in 3 Women in the U.S. Feels Discouraged About Her Finances," CreditKarma.com, October 4, 2018, https://www.creditkarma.com/insights/i/one-in-three-women-discouraged-finances-survey.

16. John Watson, "Failure Rates for Female-Controlled Businesses: Are They Any Different?" *Journal of Small Business Management,* July 2003, https://www.researchgate.net/publication/227846589_Failure_Rates_for_Female-Controlled_Businesses_Are_They_Any_Different.

17. Kerry Hannon, "8 Ways Women Entrepreneurs Can Use Crowdfunding Successfully," National Association of Women Business Owners, June 11, 2018, https://www.nawbo.org/los-angeles/nawbo-news/8-ways-women-entrepreneurs-can-use-crowdfunding-successfully.

18. Home page, Kickstarter.com.

19. Anita Roddick, AZQuotes.com, https://www.azquotes.com/quote/572573.

20. @BarbaraCorcoran, March 3, 2018, https://twitter.com/barbaracorcoran/status/969953095819120641.

21. Estee Lauder Quotes, Quoteswise.com, http://www.quoteswise.com/estee-lauder-quotes-2.html.

22. Thomas Phelps, "Lessons to Learn from Women in Sales," *The Balance Careers,* November 26, 2019, https://www.thebalancecareers.com/ms-sales-professional-2918372.

23. Marissa Mayer Quotes, BrainyQuote.com, https://www.brainyquote.com/authors/marissa-mayer-quotes.

24. Isah Aliyu Abdullahi and Pardeep Kumar, "Gender Differences in Prosocial Behaviour," *International Journal of Indian Psychology,* July 2016, https://www.researchgate.net/publication/305195572_Gender_Differences_in_Prosocial_Behaviour.

Mindset Shift 2

1. Matt Mansfield, "Startup Statistics—The Numbers You Need to Know," *Small Business Trends,* last updated June 21, 2020, https://smallbiztrends.com/2019/03/startup-statistics-small-business.html.

2. Michael Deane, "Top 6 Reasons New Businesses Fail," *Investopedia,* last updated Feb. 28, 2020, https://www.investopedia.com/financial-edge/1010/top-6-reasons-new-businesses-fail.aspx.

3. Margie Warrell, "Do Your Know Your Why? 4 Questions to Find Your Purpose," *Forbes,* last updated October 30, 2013, https://www.forbes.com/sites/margiewarrell/2013/10/30/know-your-why-4-questions-to-tap-the-power-of-purpose/#5958c90573ad;, Friedrich Nietzsche, *Brainy Quotes,* https://www.brainyquote.com/quotes/friedrich_nietzsche_103819.

4. Angela Lee Duckworth, Goodreads.com, https://www.goodreads.com/author/quotes/15454659.Angela_Lee_Duckworth

5. Eileen Fisher, *Made of Money,* https://itsamoneything.com/money/eileen-fisher-fulfilling-work-passion/.

6. Angela Duckworth, interviewed on "Who's Grittier? Men or Women?" *Daily Motion,* Sept. 1, 2016, https://www.dailymotion.com/video/x4rfdkf.

7. "Men Owned Businesses vs. Women Owned Businesses. Are There Differences?" *COFCO*, May 1, 2017, https://www.cofcogroup.com/men-owned-businesses-vs -women-owned-businesses-are-there-differences/; John Watson, "Failure Rates for Female-Controlled Businesses: Are They Any Different?" *Journal of Small Business Management*, July 2003, https://onlinelibrary.wiley.com/doi/abs/10.1111/1540 -627X.00081.

8. Marguerite Ward, "A Psychologist Says This Is the Formula for Success," CNBC.com, July 7, 2016, https://www.cnbc.com/2016/07/07/a-psychologist-says-this-is-the -formula-for-success.html.

9. Oprah Winfrey, Goodreads.com, https://www.goodreads.com/quotes/134176-think -like-a-queen-a-queen-if-not-afraid-to.

10. Meredith Lepore, "7 Pieces of Advice from Business Mogul (and Birthday Girl) Tory Burch," Instyle.com, June 17, 2015, https://www.instyle.com/news/tory-burch -inspiring-quotes.

11. Mousumi Saha Kumar, "Estée Lauder: I Never Dreamed About Success; I Just Worked for It," BrainPick.com, February 27, 2013, http://brainprick.com/estee-lauder-i-never -dreamed-about-success-i-just-worked-for-it/.

12. Thekla Morgenroth, Cordelia Fine, Michelle K. Ryan, and Anna E. Genat, "Sex, Drugs, and Reckless Driving: Are Measures Biased Toward Identifying Risk-Taking in Men?" *Social Psychological and Personality Science* 9, no. 6 (2017), https://journals.sagepub .com/doi/full/10.1177/1948550617722833.

13. KMPG, *Women's Leadership Study: Risk, Resilience Reward 2019*, https://info.kpmg.us /content/dam/info/en/news-perspectives/pdf/2019/KPMG_Womens_Leadership _Study.pdf.

14. Laura Hay, "Getting Comfortable Being Uncomfortable," KPMG.com, March 8, 2019, https://home.kpmg/xx/en/blogs/home/posts/2019/03/michele-meyer-shipp-talks -about-getting-comfortable-being-uncomfortable.html.

15. Maya Angelou, Goodreads.com, https://www.goodreads.com/author/quotes/3503 .Maya_Angelou.

16. Y. Deng, L. Chang, M. Yang, M. Huo, and R. Zhuo, "Gender Differences in Emotional Response: Inconsistencies Between Experience and Expressivity," *PLoS One* 11, no. 6 (2016):e0158666, doi:10.1371/journal.pone.0158666.

17. Gayle King, Inspiringquotes.us, https://www.inspiringquotes.us/author/7264-gayle -king.

18. "49 Best Quotes on Feedback," *Cognology*, https://cognology.com.au/49-best-quotes -on-feedback/.

19. Christina Pazzanese, "Women Less Inclined to Self-Promote Than Men, Even for a Job," *The Harvard Gazette*, February 7, 2020, https://news.harvard.edu/gazette/story /2020/02/men-better-than-women-at-self-promotion-on-job-leading-to-inequities/.

20. Katy Perry, BrainyQuote.com, https://www.brainyquote.com/quotes/katy_perry _465617

21. Brent Gleeson, "The Current Rise Of Women Entrepreneurial Leaders," Forbes.com, https://www.forbes.com/sites/brentgleeson/2019/03/08/the-current-rise-of-female -entrepreneurial-leaders/?sh=535cdca63548

22. Aimee Lee Ball, "Women and the Negativity Receptor," Oprah.com, August 2008, https://www.oprah.com/omagazine/why-women-have-low-self-esteem-how-to-feel -more-confident/all.

23. Jack Nasher, "To Seem More Competent, Be More Confident," *Harvard Business Review,* March 11, 2019, https://hbr.org/2019/03/to-seem-more-competent-be-more-confident.

24. Tara Sophia Mohr, "Why Women Don't Apply for Jobs Unless They're 100% Qualified," *Harvard Business Review,* August 25, 2014, https://hbr.org/2014/08/why-women-dont-apply-for-jobs-unless-theyre-100-qualified.

25. "Sheryl Sandberg Biography," Biography.com, updated February 5, 2020, https://www.biography.com/business-figure/sheryl-sandberg.

26. Tenacity, Dictionary.com, https://www.dictionary.com/browse/tenacity?s=t; persistence, Dictionary.com, https://www.dictionary.com/browse/persistence?s=t.

27. Mary Kay Ash, Brainyquotes.com, https://www.brainyquote.com/authors/mary-kay-ash-quotes

28. Pauline Rose Clance and Suzanne Ament Imes, "The Impostor Phenomenon In High Achieving Women: Dynamics And Therapeutic Intervention," *Psychotherapy,* 15, no. 3 (Fall 1978), https://mpowir.org/wp-content/uploads/2010/02/Download-IP-in-High-Achieving-Women.pdf.

29. Abigail Abrams, "Yes, Impostor Syndrome Is Real. Here's How to Deal with It," *Time,* last updated June 20, 2018, https://time.com/5312483/how-to-deal-with-impostor-syndrome/.

30. Jessica Bennet, "How to Overcome Impostor Syndrome," *The New York Times,* n.d., https://www.nytimes.com/guides/working-womans-handbook/overcome-impostor-syndrome.

31. Kristen Weir, "Feel Like a Fraud?" *GradPsych* 11 (2013), https://www.apa.org/gradpsych/2013/11/fraud.

32. Abrams, "Yes, Impostor Syndrome Is Real."

33. Leslie Feinzaig, "Female Founders Need to Stop Self-Sabotaging," Entrepreneur.com, October 23, 2018, https://www.entrepreneur.com/article/321758.

34. Arianna Huffington, Brainyquotes.com, https://www.brainyquote.com/quotes/arianna_huffington_396029.

Mindset Shift 3

1. Marc Pearlman, "Is Your Money Mindset Crippling Your Company?" Entrepreneur.com, June 29, 2010, https://www.entrepreneur.com/article/207266.

2. Laura Huang, "Why Female Entrepreneurs Have a Harder Time Raising Venture Capital," *Scientific American,* June 5, 2018, https://www.scientificamerican.com/article/why-female-entrepreneurs-have-a-harder-time-raising-venture-capital1/.

3. Katherine M. Dean, "Common Money Mindset Hurdles for Women," *Opal Wealth Advisors,* April 24, 2019, https://opalwealthadvisors.com/blog/common-money-mindset-hurdles-for-women/.

4. T. Harv Eker, *Secrets of the Millionaire Mind* (New York: Harper, 2000).

5. Cameron Huddleston, "Americans Are Living Their Worst Financial Nightmares, Survey Finds," GoBankingRates.com, July 26, 2017, https://www.gobankingrates.com/investing/strategy/americas-3-biggest-money-fears-how-overcome/.

6. Dave Ramsey, "How to Stop Living Paycheck to Paycheck," March 2020, *Ramsey,* https://www.daveramsey.com/blog/stop-living-paycheck-to-paycheck.

7. Kerry Hannon, "What's Different Financially for Women?" *Merrill Lynch,* https://www.ml.com/articles/whats-different-financially-for-women.html.

8. Northwestern Mutual, *Elements of Success Survey*, 2014, https://news .northwesternmutual.com/elements-of-success-study-2014.

9. *Women and Financial Wellness: Beyond the Bottom Line*, Age Wave and Merrill Lynch, accessed February 2020, https://agewave.com/what-we-do/landmark-research-and -consulting/research-studies/women-and-financial-wellness/.

10. Suze Orman, *Women and Money* (New York: Spiegel and Grau, 2010).

11. Lakshmi Balachandra, "Beyond the Bucks," Babson College, https://www.babson.edu /academics/centers-and-institutes/center-for-womens-entrepreneurial-leadership /diana-international-research-institute/research/beyond-the-bucks/#.

12. Friederike Mengel, "Gender Differences in Networking," *The Economic Journal*, July 28, 2015, https://pdfs.semanticscholar.org/d486/bdaba1fe19f9235d02d4238a355 71273bf3d.pdf.

13. Hilla Dotan, "Women Are As Good As Men When Negotiating for Friends," *Biospace*, September 8, 2016, https://www.biospace.com/article/around-the-web/women -are-as-good-as-men-when-negotiating-for-friends-tel-aviv-university-study-/; Benjamin Artz, Amanda Goodall, and Andrew J. Oswald, "Research: Women Ask for Raises as Often as Men but Are Less Likely to Get Them," *Harvard Business Review*, June 25, 2018, https://hbr.org/2018/06/research-women-ask-for-raises-as-often-as -men-but-are-less-likely-to-get-them.

14. Sheryl Sandberg, "Policies to Promote Women's Economic Opportunities," *The Hamilton Project*, October 19, 2017, https://www.hamiltonproject.org/events /policies_to_promote_womens_economic_opportunity?utm_campaign=Economic %20Studies&utm_source=hs_email&utm_medium=email&utm_content=57439024.

15. Victoria Medvec, "Five Ways That Women Can Negotiate More Effectively," Kellogg Insight, last updated March 1, 2018, https://insight.kellogg.northwestern.edu/article /five-ways-women-can-negotiate-more-effectively.

16. Diana Farrell, Christopher Wheat, and Chi Mac, *Gender, Age and Small Business Financial Outcomes*, JP Morgan Chase, February 2019, https://institute.jpmorganchase.com /content/dam/jpmc/jpmorgan-chase-and-co/institute/pdf/institute-report-small -business-financial-outcomes.pdf.

17. Gary Stockton, "Statistics and Obstacles Facing Women Entrepreneurs," Experian .com, January 29, 2018, https://www.experian.com/blogs/small-business-matters /2018/01/29/statistics-and-obstacles-facing-women-entrepreneurs/.

18. "Do Women Have a Harder Time Securing Funding?" *Capital One*, last modified August 3, 2020, https://www.capitalone.com/about/newsroom/do-women-have -harder-time-securing-capital/.

19. "Small Business Growth Index," *Capital One*, accessed February 2020, https://www .capitalone.com/small-business/credit-cards/small-business-growth-index/.

Mindset Shift 4

1. Kim Parker, "Despite Progress, Women Still Bear Heavier Load than Men in Balancing Work and Family," Pew Research Center, March 10, 2015, https://www.pewresearch .org/fact-tank/2015/03/10/women-still-bear-heavier-load-than-men-balancing -work-family/.

2. Letecia Gasca, "Why Do Low Income Entrepreneurs Fail? New Research Provides Some Answers," NextBillion.net, February 28, 2018, https://nextbillion.net/why-do -low-income-women-entrepreneurs-fail-new-research-provides-some-answers/.

3. A.W. Geiger, Gretchen Livingston, and Kristin Bialik, "6 Facts About U.S. Moms," Pew Research Center, May 8, 2019, https://www.pewresearch.org/fact-tank/2019/05/08/facts-about-u-s-mothers/.

4. Barbara De Angelis, Goodreads.com, https://www.goodreads.com/author/quotes/72891.Barbara_De_Angelis.

5. L. Torstveit, S. Sütterlin, and R.G. Lugo, "Empathy, Guilt Proneness and Gender: Relative Contributions to Prosocial Behavior," *Europe's Journal of Psychology* 12, no. 2 (2016): 260–270, https://doi.org/10.5964/ejop.v12i2.1097.

6. Michelle Obama, Brainyquotes.com, https://www.brainyquote.com/quotes/michelle_obama_411952.

7. Margaret Thatcher, BrainyQuotes.com, https://www.brainyquote.com/quotes/margaret_thatcher_127088.

Mindset Shift 5

1. Christina Pazzanese, "Women Less Inclined to Self-Promote Than Men, Even for a Job," *The Harvard Gazette,* last modified February 7, 2020, https://news.harvard.edu/gazette/story/2020/02/menbetter-than-women-at-self-promotion-on-job-leading-to-inequities/.

2. Sophia Dembling, "Are Men Better at Selling Themselves?," *GradPsych* 11 (2011):45, https://www.apa.org/gradpsych/2011/11/cover-men.

3. Dorie Clarke, "How Women Can Develop and Promote Their Personal Brand," *Harvard Business Review,* last modified March 2, 2018, https://hbr.org/2018/03/how-women-can-develop-and-promote-their-personal-brand.

4. Tom Peters, "The Brand Called You," *Fast Company*, August 31, 1997, https://www.fastcompany.com/28905/brand-called-you.

5. Sunil Kataria, "Do People Buy Goods and Services or Stories and Magic?," *The Economic Times,* last updated February 7, 2017, https://economictimes.indiatimes.com/do-people-buy-goods-and-services-or-stories-and-magic/articleshow/57016683.cms?from=mdr.

6. Zig Zigler, Quotable Quotes, Goodreads.com, https://www.goodreads.com/quotes/908071-if-people-like-you-they-ll-listen-to-you-but-if.

7. Brené Brown, Quotable Quotes, Goodreads.com, https://www.goodreads.com/quotes/625801-courage-starts-with-showing-up-and-letting-ourselves-be-seen.

Mindset Shift 6

1. "Most Popular Social Media Sites Review: Why Women Are the Real Power Behind the Success of Pinterest and Tumblr," *Finances Online*, https://reviews.financesonline.com/most-popular-social-media-sites-review/; Iris Vermeren, "Men vs. Women: Who Is More Active on Social Media?" January 28, 2015, https://www.brandwatch.com/blog/men-vs-women-active-social-media/.

2. Brent Barnhart, "The Most Important Social Media Trends to Know for 2020," *Sprout Social*, https://sproutsocial.com/insights/social-media-trends/.

3. "These Are the Most Authentic Brands of 2017," *Social Media Week*, last updated October 25, 2017, https://socialmediaweek.org/blog/2017/10/authentic-brands-2017/.

4. Jonah Berger and Katherine Milkman, "What Makes Online Content Viral?," *Journal of Marketing Research*, December 25, 2009, https://papers.ssrn.com/sol3/papers.cfm?abstract_id=1528077.

5. "New Cone Communications Research Confirms Millennials as America's Most Ardent CSR Supporters," press release, *Cone*, September 23, 2015, https://www .conecomm.com/news-blog/new-cone-communications-research-confirms -millennials-as-americas-most-ardent-csr-supporters.

6. Ibid.

7. Barnhart, "The Most Important Social Media Trends to Know for 2020."

8. James Wright, Davitha Ghiassi, Mark Campbell, Racheal Sampon, and Jackie Crossman, *Red Sky Predictions: 10 Predictions for Communicators in 2020*, Red Havas, https://redhavas.com/wp-content/uploads/2020/02/RedSkyPredictions_2020.pdf.

9. "20 Influencer Marketing Statistics That Will Surprise You," *Digital Marketing Institute*, https://digitalmarketinginstitute.com/en-us/blog/20-influencer-marketing -statistics-that-will-surprise-you.

10. Barnhart, "The Most Important Social Media Trends to Know for 2020."

11. Allison Pfaff, "Get Inspired by These 11 Standout Quotes from Content Marketing Experts and Creators," *The Story Studio*, August 8, 2019, https://www .hearststorystudio.com/blog/get-inspired-by-these-11-standout-quotes-from -content-marketing-experts-and-creators.

12. "GoodFirms New Study: Around 67% of People Unfollow Brands on Social Media Due to Irrelevant Content," July 31, 2019, *Ciston PR Newswire*, https://www.prnewswire .com/news-releases/goodfirms-new-study-around-67-of-people-unfollow-brands-on -social-media-due-to-irrelevant-content-300893966.html.

Mindset Shift 7

1. Juntae DeLane, "How Do Men & Women Use Social Media," *Digital Branding Institute*, https://digitalbrandinginstitute.com/how-do-men-women-use-social-media/.

2. Olga Rabo, "The 10 Most Used Instagram Filters," Iconosquare.com, last updated on August 19, 2020, https://blog.iconosquare.com/top-10-instagram-filters/.

3. Ella Woodward Quotes, BrainyQuote.com, https://www.brainyquote.com/authors /ella-woodward-quotes.

4. Gigi Hadid, QuoteCites.com, https://quotecites.com/quotes/gigi-hadid-4303/.

5. "Number of Facebook Users Worldwide from 2015 to 2020," *Statista*, https://www .statista.com/statistics/490424/number-of-worldwide-facebook-users/.

6. Elizabeth Arens, "The Best Times to Post on Social Media in 2020," last updated on August 3, 2020, https://sproutsocial.com/insights/best-times-to-post-on-social -media/#fb-times.

7. Quotes about Social Media Branding, *Quote Master*, https://www.quotemaster.org /social+media+branding.

8. "Distribution of TikTok Users in the United States as of June 2020, by Age Group," *Statista*, https://www.statista.com/statistics/1095186/tiktok-us-users-age/.

9. "Snapchat by the Numbers: Stats, Demographics, & Fun Facts," *Omnicore*, last updated February 7, 2020, https://www.omnicoreagency.com/snapchat-statistics/.

10. "Pinterest by the Numbers: Stats, Demographics, & Fun Facts," *Omnicore*, last updated July 29, 2020, https://www.omnicoreagency.com/pinterest-statistics/.

11. "Pinterest by the Numbers: Stats, Demographics, & Fun Facts," *Omnicore*, last updated July 29, 2020, https://www.omnicoreagency.com/pinterest-statistics/.

12. "YouTube.com September 2020 Overview," *Similar Web*, https://www.similarweb.com /website/youtube.com/.

13. Germany Kent, LinkedIn Quotes, Goodreads.com, https://www.goodreads.com /quotes/tag/linkedin.

Mindset Shift 8

1. "The State of Small Business: 2019 Women in Business Trends and Statistics," *Guidant Financial*, http://www.guidantfinancial.com/resources/2019-women-in-business -trends-and-statistics/.
2. "Barriers & Bias: The Status of Women in Leadership," American Association of University Women, https://www.aauw.org/resources/research/barrier-bias/.
3. Matthew Biddle, "Men Are Still More Likely Than Women to Be Perceived as Leaders, Study Finds," *University at Buffalo News Center*, August 6, 2018, http://www.buffalo .edu/news/news-releases.host.html/content/shared/mgt/news/men-still-more -likely-than-women-perceived-leaders-study-finds.detail.html.
4. "Campaigner Personality," *16 Personalities*, https://www.16personalities.com/enfp -conclusion.
5. Dolly Parton, Quotable Quotes, Goodreads.com, https://www.goodreads.com/quotes /39182-if-your-actions-create-a-legacy-that-inspires-others-to.
6. Maya Angelou, BrainyQuote.com, https://www.brainyquote.com/quotes/maya _angelou_392897.
7. Beyoncé Knowles, BrainyQuote.com, https://www.brainyquote.com/authors /beyonce-knowles-quotes.

Mindset Shift 9

1. Rita Zahara Quotes and Sayings, *Inspiring Quotes*, https://www.inspiringquotes.us /author/4236-rita-zahara/page:2.
2. Henry David Thoreau, BrainyQuote.com, https://www.brainyquote.com/authors /henry-david-thoreau-quotes.
3. Helen Keller Quotes, AZQuotes.com, https://www.azquotes.com/author/7843 -Helen_Keller.
4. Marian Diamond Quotes, AZQuotes.com, https://www.azquotes.com/author/26544 -Marian_Diamond.

Mindset Shift 10

1. Eva de Mol, Jeff Pollack, and Violet T. Ho, "What Makes Entrepreneurs Burn Out," *Harvard Business Review*, April 4, 2018, https://hbr.org/2018/04/what-makes -entrepreneurs-burn-out.
2. Margaret M. Quinn and Peter M. Smith, "Gender, Work, and Health," *Annals of Work Exposures and Health* 62, no. 4 (2018), https://academic.oup.com/annweh/article/62 /4/389/4956148.
3. Thomas E. Rojo Aubrey, Quotable Quote, Goodreads.com, https://www.goodreads .com/quotes/9884622-dear-stress-i-would-like-a-divorce-please-understand-it.
4. McKenzie Jean-Philippe, "25 Oprah Quotes that Have All the Wisdom You'll Ever Need," *O, The Oprah Magazine*, May 22, 2019, https://www.oprahmag.com/life /g23429862/oprah-quotes/.

INDEX

ABOUT THE AUTHOR

Charlene Walters is an entrepreneurship coach, business and branding mentor, author, and trainer. She developed a digital entrepreneurship MBA program, serves as a mentor on *Entrepreneur* magazine's "Ask an Expert" forum and through her own consulting business (www .charlenewalters.com); is featured among other CEOs, influencers, and celebrities on the BAM Network; and was selected as one of 150 Marketers to Follow by Rubicly. In addition to her entrepreneurial endeavors, Charlene has held a variety of sales, management, and marketing roles at startups and larger corporations.

Charlene enjoys combining her knowledge and love of marketing and business strategy with her passion for innovation and desire to help others succeed—working with entrepreneurs to launch their startups, hone their personal brands, and further their business strategies and entrepreneurial goals.

In addition to *Launch Your Inner Entrepreneur*, Charlene wrote a slice-of-life memoir about overcoming tragedy and loss and moving forward in life, based on her own personal experience when her husband passed away unexpectedly when her daughters were only two and four years old. As part of that, she serves as a speaker and mentor to others, and writes and contributes to numerous publications on business and motivational topics. You can find Charlene quoted in media outlets including *Entrepreneur* magazine, *Woman's Day*, *Redbook*, *UpJourney*, *Fupping*, *Bustle*, *Business Insider*, *Business News Daily*, *Best Life*, *Authority Magazine*, *Thrive Global*, *Women's Health*, *Martha Stewart*, *Forbes* and many others. Charlene also writes a blog called *Entrepreneurship, Life Enthusiasm & Energizing Your Brand* and has taught hundreds of business, marketing, and entrepreneurship courses and workshops for businesses and universities. She has also appeared in or on many videos, podcasts, and blogs.

Charlene has a BA in English, an MBA in management, and a PhD in business administration/marketing. She is a busy single parent, women's empowerment advocate, fan of kayaking, fitness, and the beach, a laughter and sunset seeker, and the very proud mother of two beautiful daughters. Charlene lives in Charlotte, North Carolina, by way of California, Florida, South Carolina, and Connecticut.

Follow Charlene on Social:

Twitter: @CWaltersPhD

Instagram: @CharleneWaltersPhD

LinkedIn: Charlene Walters, PhD

Visit her website/subscribe to her blog:

www.charlenewalters.com

Follow her on Amazon:

www.amazon.com/Charlene-Walters/e/B08J4HBH6F/